On
Being Authentic

Praise for the series

"... allows a space for distinguished thinkers to write about their passions."

The Philosophers' Magazine

"... deserves high praise."

Boyd Tonkin, The Independent (UK)

"This is clearly an important series. I look forward to reading future volumes."

Frank Kermode, author of Shakespeare's Language

"... both rigorous and accessible."

Humanist News

"... the series looks superb."

Quentin Skinner

"... an excellent and beautiful series."

Ben Rogers, author of A.J. Ayer: A Life

"Routledge's *Thinking in Action* series is the theory junkie's answer to the eminently pocketable Penguin 60s series."

Mute Magazine (UK)

"Routledge's new series, *Thinking in Action*, brings philosophers to our aid ..."

Evening Standard (UK)

"... a welcome new series by Routledge."

Bulletin of Science, Technology and Society

CHARLES GUIGNON

On
Being Authentic

Routledge
Taylor & Francis Group
LONDON AND NEW YORK

First published 2004
by Routledge
2 Park Square, Milton Park, Abingdon, Oxon, OX14 4RN

Simultaneously published in the USA and Canada
by Routledge
711 Third Avenue, New York, NY 10017

Routledge is an imprint of the Taylor & Francis Group, an informa business

© 2004 Charles Guignon

Typeset in Joanna MT by
RefineCatch Ltd, Bungay, Suffolk

British Library Cataloguing in Publication Data
A catalogue record for this book is available from the British Library

Library of Congress Cataloging in Publication Data
Guignon, Charles B., 1944–
  On being authentic / Charles Guignon. – 1st ed.
    p.   cm. – (Thinking in action)
  Includes bibliographical references.
  1. Authenticity (Philosophy) 2. Self-realization. I. Title. II. Series.
  B105.A8G85 2004
  128 – dc22   2003027596

ISBN10: 0–415–26122–8 hbk
ISBN10: 0–415–26123–6 pbk

ISBN13: 978–0–415–26122–7 hbk
ISBN13: 978–0–415–26123–4 pbk

Preface

The subject matter of this book has been close to my heart for many years. My first encounter with what we now call "self-help" movements was in my childhood home a half century ago. My mother was devoted to the works of such inspirational writers as Dale Carnegie and Norman Vincent Peale, and she saw to it that our family benefited from the sermonettes of Bishop Fulton J. Sheen on television each week. Among my earliest memories are those of my mother attempting to cure me of my "negative attitudes" by reminding me of the power of positive thinking. With tireless effort she struggled to set my sister and me off on a life dedicated to winning friends and influencing people.

Being counter-suggestible by nature, I of course rebelled against the whole business. By the late fifties and early sixties, I was immersing myself in the newly translated writings of existentialist thinkers, absorbed not in positive thinking and winning friends but in anxiety, ennui, anguish, being-unto-death, and l'homme révolté. But even though the orientation was different, the concern with understanding what life can and should be remained my central interest in philosophy. Over the years I have come to owe a special debt of gratitude to my teachers and guides, above all Bert Dreyfus, Alasdair MacIntyre, Richard Rorty and Charles Taylor, whose thought about these matters has provided the foundation for my own work.

My interest in the self-help ideas circulating in popular culture was sparked again recently when I met and married a woman who, having for years been involved in New Age and self-improvement programs, was now quite critical of these movements. With her, I began to watch Oprah and later Dr. Phil on television, and to think through the ideas underlying pop psychology and the self-help industry. From all the ideas circulating in this vast field, I have taken one particular notion to serve as the topic for this book: the idea of authenticity. This is a book about the ideal of being an authentic individual.

It could be argued that the ideal of authentic existence is absolutely central to all the movements that make up the self-improvement culture. As we shall see in Chapter 1, many of the most influential writers in this tradition either explicitly or implicitly make reference to the project of becoming authentic in their writings. But the ideal is of interest not just to New Age writers. Philosophers from widely different orientations have also directed their thought to this topic. A variety of thinkers who have been influenced by the twentieth-century German philosopher Martin Heidegger have tried to work through the concept as it is developed in his work.[1] Coming from a very different tradition, the English philosopher, Bernard Williams, expressed the centrality of authenticity to his thought this way: "If there's one theme in all my work it's about authenticity and self-expression. It's the idea that some things are in some real sense really you, or express what you are, and others aren't."[2]

Another influential philosopher who contributes to current reflection on the notion of authenticity is Stanley Cavell of Harvard. Though he does not make much use of the word "authenticity," the concept is clearly central to his account of "moral perfectionism," an approach to moral thought that is, he says, "directed less to restraining the bad than to releasing the good."[3] Writing on the philosophy of Emerson, Nietzsche and Cavell, the American philosopher Russell Goodman defines "moral perfectionism" as an approach to moral philosophy "in which the idea of the individual being true to, cultivating, or developing him- or herself occupies a central place."[4] The concept of moral perfectionism was already formulated by Cavell's hero, Ralph Waldo Emerson, who in "Self-Reliance" wrote: "Nothing is sacred but the integrity of your own mind. . . . No law can be sacred to me but that of my nature. Good and bad are but names very transferable to that or this; the only right is what is after my constitution, the only wrong what is against it."[5]

As is the case for just about all the ideas promoted by self-help gurus and motivational speakers, there is obviously something clearly right about the ideal of authenticity. In the final chapter of this book, I will try to show what I take to be some of the advantages of authenticity regarded as a personal and social virtue. Nevertheless, the primary aim of this book is not to sing the praises of authenticity, but to put in question some of the unstated assumptions that surround it and prop it up.

My criticism of the ideal of authenticity reflects my overall response to the output of the self-help culture. What fascinates me about this culture is how its exponents succeed in illuminating some very important dimensions of life, but in doing so often conceal or cover up other aspects of life that are just as important. The problem with self-help ideas is not that they are wrong, but that they are one-sided. That is why latching on to them as if they were the answer to your problems cuts you off from a sensitivity to other virtues and ideals that are not only equally good, but are absolutely essential to living a meaningful and fulfilling life. The one-sidedness of these ideals explains why many people who buy into them end up feeling frustrated and defeated, unable to understand why such a good program of self-improvement turned out to be so disappointing. Followers of the New Age culture often respond to this disappointment by latching on to a new set of ideas or a new guru, feverishly pursuing this new path for a while, only to once again end up feeling frustrated and let down. And so on in an endless cycle. It is because of the way they lead to obsessive, almost addictive immersion in ever renewed self-improvement projects that New Age culture and self-help programs have gained a reputation for leading to excessive self-absorption – the "me, me, me" culture so deliciously skewered by the social critic Tom Wolfe three decades ago.[6]

Part of the appeal of the ideal of authenticity comes from the fact that the notion grows out of a tradition of practices and thought that have been profoundly important in Western civilization. In Chapter 2, we will look at two especially important versions of this tradition. But for now, we may simply note the existence of an important religious tradition in our world that directs us to look inward and make contact with an inner truth in order to gain guidance for our lives. This tradition came to a head in the writings and teachings of late medieval and early modern religious reformers who criticized the authoritarian and dogmatic tendencies of the established Church and insisted that human beings must find guidance on the basis of their own conscience in a one-to-one relation to God.

The upshot of this reformist development was a conception of the religious life emphasizing the idea that "the Kingdom of God is within you," the idea that each of us can and should find God within ourselves. This is the message conveyed by the oft-quoted words of the early seventeenth-century theologian and mystic, William Law:

> Though God is everywhere present, yet He is only present to thee in the deepest and most central part of thy soul. The natural senses cannot possess God or unite thee to Him; nay, thy inward faculties of understanding, will and memory can only reach after God, but cannot be the place of his habitation in thee. But there is a root or depth of thee from whence all these faculties come forth, as lines from a center, or as branches from the body of the tree. This depth is called the center, the fund or bottom of the soul. This depth is the unity, the eternity – I had almost said the infinity – of thy soul; for it is so infinite that nothing can satisfy it or give it rest but the infinity of God.[7]

Given such an image of the God within, the project of turning inward to find guidance and ultimate truth seems self-evident. Charles Taylor has shown in some detail how religious ideas have become central to the understanding of the self we now share in the modern world.[8]

Contemporary self-help gurus are acutely aware of their connection to this religious tradition. In an especially telling passage, Dr. Phil McGraw, a pivotal figure we will meet again in Chapter 1, describes his "old-fashioned" commitments as follows: "I hold the rather old-fashioned belief that each of us is blessed with particular gifts given to us by God, and that it is our sacred obligation to identify, to cherish, and to exercise those gifts for the betterment of ourselves and of those in our lives."[9] And Oprah Winfrey, without doubt the most influential personality in the self-transformation movement, displays her religious orientation when she says, "I have church with myself: I have church walking down the street. I believe in the God force that lives inside all of us, and once you tap into that, you can do anything." Like Dr. Phil, she experiences her life's work as a response to God's calling: "I am guided by a higher calling. It's not so much a voice as it is a feeling. If it doesn't feel right to me, I don't do it."[10]

Further evidence for the religious origins of these ideas is found in the appearance of the word "spirituality" in practically every area of the self-help and inspirational literature. We learn that everyday life is spiritual, that there is spirituality in little things, that life is a spiritual quest, and so on and on, usually in a way that is oblivious of the fact that the word "spirituality" as now used is a relatively recent invention, having a clear meaning only in relation to specifically modern conceptions of the aims of life.[11]

What is at issue, however, is not whether self-help gurus are connected to a long and rich religious tradition. It is, instead, whether the ideals and ways of thinking that originally made sense within that religious tradition are still meaningful when taken out of that tradition and planted in the secularized soil of modernity. When God becomes a sort of afterthought, or when the "God within" comes to be thought of simply as God's *being me*, then the context of ideas in which the practice of inward-turning and expressing the true self originally made sense undergoes a profound change. What is lost, among other things, is the notion of an authoritative source of direction and insight I can turn to in order to learn how I should live my life. For when my guide is understood as nothing other than me, it is hard to see what authority this guidance could or should have. Moreover, as we shall see, the very notion of an intrinsically good, substantial self lying within becomes increasingly problematic in the contemporary world. The joint caustic effects of doubt, critical reflection and science have dissolved the conceptual web in which the ideal of self-discovery and being true to one's own self originally made sense. As a result, all we have today is bits and pieces of old ideas found among the scattered debris of past traditions, ideas that are patched together to form a picture of what life is all about. With respect to the notion of authenticity, I shall argue, this picture really does not make much sense.

My method in this book is to trace the historical development of the concept of authenticity from its origins in the eighteenth century to its problematic uses today. Given that this is intended to be a relatively short book, the story must be rather coarse and schematic, making bald assertions about historical outlooks with no appreciation of the complexities of the historical record. I hope that the story is roughly on target even if it is not always accurate in its details. A much more detailed and carefully wrought version of this story is available in Charles Taylor's classic work, *Sources of the Self*, and in his more abridged account, *The Ethics of Authenticity*.[12] I would think my little book was a success if it led readers to read Taylor's more extensive discussions.

As I am always struck at first by what is right about an idea, I generally proceed by making the best possible case for the particular view I am examining, and only then going on to raise criticisms or doubts about it. I mention this because it sometimes can be a bit maddening to be led to think that the view under consideration is surely the right one, only to find it roundly trounced a couple of pages later. Maddening though it may be, however, there is something to be said for getting inside a view and getting a feel for its appeal before going on to look at what is wrong with it. Only when we understand why intelligent people hold a position can we see what is at stake in attacking it.

I owe a debt of gratitude to a number of people who read and commented on parts of this book or discussed its ideas with me over the years. In addition to my teachers mentioned above, I am indebted to Kevin Aho, Tony Bruce, Russell Goodman, Chioke I'Anson, Richard Kearney, Frank Richardson, Phil Sinaikin, Frank-M. Staemmler, and Polly Young-Eisendrath. Generations of students in my Philosophy in Literature and Film and Philosophy of Psychotherapy courses also have made immeasurable contributions to this book. I wish I could identify each one by name. Finally, and most of all, I must thank my wife, Sally Guignon, for the stimulating conversations and steady encouragement that made this book possible.

One

"Authentic Life Design™ was founded on the belief that authentic people are happy, joyous and free – and that each of us can make the choice for authenticity. We believe that knowing who we are and being those people is the best life has to offer – and we are committed to this end." So begins the home page of an American web site that speaks to the most heartfelt dreams and aspirations of many people today. In books, television talk shows and magazine articles, the idea of achieving an authentic existence arises on a daily basis. Oprah Winfrey has made authenticity a central theme for her six or seven million daily viewers, showcasing such self-help gurus as Gary Zukav, author of *The Seat of the Soul*, and Phillip C. McGraw, whose *Self Matters: Creating Your Life from the Inside Out* dominated the *New York Times* self-help bestseller list for months.[1]

McGraw – "Dr. Phil" as he is known to the millions of viewers who have seen him on *Oprah* and on his own daily show – is especially dynamic in his sales pitch for authenticity. He frankly admits that he used to be a "sellout," a person who caved in to social expectations and money, was trapped in "life-chain momentum," and ignored his own voice, needs and passions. Then, on a beautiful afternoon, he realized that his "life absolutely sucked," that he hated his career, hated his house, and hated himself for getting so deep into it that he now felt like he couldn't get out. At that moment he resolved to "totally reengineer those parts of my life that were not 'me,' and build on those that felt right because they *were* right."[2] Dr. Phil's exceptional appeal lies in the fact that his conversion experience resonates with the most troubling experiences of many of those in his audience. A modern-day Paul on the road to Damascus, he sees it all in a moment of vision: "I have one shot at this, one shot, and I'm choking, I'm blowing it. I'm now almost forty years old. I've wasted ten years of my life and I can't get them back no matter what I do" (p. 6).

But unlike the conversion experiences of such historical figures as St. Paul, St. Augustine or Martin Luther, Dr. Phil's moment of vision presents him not with an understanding of his relation to God, but of his relation to himself. "So, what is this authentic self I keep talking about?" he asks, and he answers:

> The authentic self is the *you* that can be found at your absolute core. It is the part of you that is not defined by your job, or your function, or your role. It is the composite of all your unique gifts, skills, abilities, interests, talents, insights, and wisdom. It is all your strengths and values that are uniquely yours and need expression, versus what you have been programmed to believe that you are "supposed to be and do." It is the you that flourished, unself-consciously, in those times in your life when you felt happiest and most fulfilled. (p. 30)

In the moment of vision, what is disclosed is not something outside yourself; rather, it is *you* yourself. Yet this *you* that is discovered is a *you* that is for the most part concealed, hidden, lost, displaced, almost totally forgotten. What is needed, then, is a project of self-transformation aimed at recovering this lost you and reinstating it to its proper place at the center of your life.

So the ideal of authenticity is a project of becoming the person you are. It might seem self-evident to us in our current world that authenticity so understood is the ultimate task of life. But the aim of life has not always been understood this way. In the self-help books of a half century ago, the project of personal transformation was generally pictured as one of becoming something you were not yet – becoming a person who is *more than* or *better than* what he or she had been before. In the age of what David Riesman called the "other-directed" individual,[3] books with titles like *How to Make Friends and Influence People* set out to make people more successful and popular by changing the way they presented themselves in everyday life. Coming from a different perspective, Norman Vincent Peale's immensely influential *The Power of Positive Thinking* promised to show the reader how to achieve happiness through ways of thinking that emphasized not self-discovery but dependence on God: "Put yourself in God's hands," Peale writes; "To do that simply state, 'I am in God's hands.' Then believe you are NOW receiving all the power you need. 'Feel' it flowing into you. Affirm that 'the kingdom of God is within you.' "[4]

These older conceptions of self-transformation presuppose a distinction between what you currently are – your uncultivated self or (as we might now say) "unevolved" self – and an image of what you can become if you become all you can be, that is, if you realize your potential and purpose as a human being. For such older conceptions, the ideal condition you strive to reach is something you have the capacity to achieve, but it is not necessarily equated with any set of traits and characteristics already in you. In contrast, the contemporary ideal of *authenticity* directs you to realize and *be* that which you *already are*, the unique, definitive traits already there within you.

The picture of pregiven but currently unfulfilled inner traits generally presupposes that we have something within us that we are now unwilling or unable to raise to expression. For the therapist Fritz Perls, the opposite of authentic existence is what he calls *neurosis*, a condition that results from the "attempt to get away from oneself." The neurotic person "has given up living for his self in a way that would actualize himself," with the result that "there is a feeling of not being alive, of deadness. We feel that we are nothing, we are things." On Perls' view, it is only by breaking out of "the phoniness of game-playing" that we can "become authentic" and so become our true selves.[5]

The promoters of authenticity generally assume that the task of being oneself is not only the primary task in life; it is the task we are best equipped to accomplish. A song by the group They Might Be Giants, tongue no doubt firmly planted in cheek, puts it this way:

> There's only one thing that I know how to do well
> And I've often been told that you can only do
> What you know how to do well
> And that's be you,
> Be what you're like,
> Be like yourself . . .[6]

But even though being who we are is our proper task in life, it is not an easy task. Everything in social existence pulls us away from being ourselves, for the simple reason that society works best by making people into cogs in the machinery of everyday life. The outer world of practical affairs runs most smoothly when people identify with their roles and fulfill their functions without questioning or running against the grain. Jean-Paul Sartre noted this about tradespeople performing their tasks in daily life: "The public demands of them that they realize [their occupations] as a ceremony: there is the dance of the grocer, of the tailor, of the auctioneer, by which they endeavor to persuade their clientele that they are nothing but a grocer, an auctioneer, a tailor. A grocer who dreams is offensive to the buyer, because such a grocer is not wholly a grocer."[7] Because social pressures pull us toward inauthentic role-playing, becoming authentic takes serious effort; it calls for spiritual exercises comparable to those to which religious initiates were formerly subjected.

A burgeoning industry has grown up in recent years with the aim of reforming and transforming people in order to make them authentic. Among the masters of the field is Thomas Moore, whose monumental bestseller *Care of the Soul* uses myth and ritual to help people recover their true selves – their souls – in order to achieve a more integrated and tranquil way of living in everyday life. Another influential writer, Deepak Chopra, draws on Indian philosophy to show his readers that "each of us is here to discover our true Self" and that each of us has "a unique talent and a unique way of expressing it."[8] Various "recovery" and self-improvement programs have taken up the ways of thinking central to the authenticity movement and made them part of their vernacular. Many of these programs are laid out as a series of "steps" one must take on the path to recovery and self-fulfillment. So Dr. Phil offers a "five-step action plan" to help people move from being a "fictional self" to being an "authentic self," Cheryl

Richardson offers a "personal coach's seven-step program" to a better life, assorted recovery programs offer twelve-step procedures, and there are other versions of step programs available to the wise shopper. For the many professional therapists who have learned from the insights of the British psychoanalyst D. W. Winnicott, the program of transformation involves therapeutic interaction aimed at freeing clients from the constricting demands of the "false self" to enable them to access and express the "true self" within.

The basic assumption built into the ideal of authenticity is that, lying within each individual, there is a deep, "true self" – the "Real Me" – in distinction from all that is not really me. This real, inner self contains the constellation of feelings, needs, desires, capacities, aptitudes, dispositions, and creative abilities that make the person a unique individual. The ideal of authenticity has two components. First, the project of becoming authentic asks us to get in touch with the real self we have within, a task that is achieved primarily through introspection, self-reflection or meditation. Only if we can candidly appraise ourselves and achieve genuine self-knowledge can we begin to realize our capacity for authentic existence. Second, this ideal calls on us to express that unique constellation of inner traits in our actions in the external world – to actually be what we are in our ways of being present in our relationships, careers, and practical activities. The assumption is that it is only by expressing our true selves that we can achieve self-realization and self-fulfillment as authentic human beings.

The idea that becoming authentic is our highest goal in life might seem so self-evident as to be not worth discussing. It is important to see, however, that there are at least two different ways one might answer the age-old question, What is the most meaningful and worthwhile life possible for humans? The first, the concept of authenticity, is an ideal of *owning* oneself, of achieving *self-possession*. Let us call such a conception of self-ownership the ideal of "enownment." It is the ideal that is associated with such motivating slogans as "Be all that you can be," or – a phrase we will look at later – "Become what you are." As we have seen, this ideal starts out from the assumption that each individual already contains resources and potentialities that are worth expressing in his or her activities in the world.

The second ideal emphasizes not enownment, but rather *self-loss* or *releasement*. This second vision of the good life urges you to look away from your own personal feelings and needs and to give your life over to something greater than yourself. It is a vision of life explored by the Russian author Dostoevsky in *The Brothers Karamazov* and other novels and stories.[9] Dostoevsky holds that the pervasive social friction and conflict in the modern world is rooted in the overweening self-centeredness and extreme individualism running through contemporary life. This self-absorption leads to a struggle for self-affirmation and personal success that pits each individual against others and in the end produces isolation and mutual contempt. The constant preoccupation with self cuts you off from others, breeding competition, aggressiveness, envy, alienation, and ultimately despair. As an alternative, Dostoevsky makes a case for the Russian ideal expressed in the Greek word *kenōsis*, the word used in the Bible to refer to Christ's self-emptying and self-abnegation. Contained in this notion is an ideal of "belongingness" or "togetherness," a conception of being part of a wider flow of life rather than being in contention with everyone else in a struggle for self-enhancement.

The model of self-loss directs you to turn your back on the self-preoccupation and self-inspection demanded by the culture of authenticity. The highest goal in living, on this view, is to become a new person by becoming responsive to the call of something greater than yourself. This "something greater" may be thought of as God's will, social solidarity and reform, the sanctified callings of ordinary life, the cosmic order of things, or even "Being" (the philosopher Heidegger said that humans are the "shepherds of Being"). The suggestion here is that we should seek release from the bondage to ego, not ever greater involvement in the "I."

Each of these views of the good life will be able to point out shortcomings in the other. From the standpoint of defenders of the ideal of authenticity, the path of self-loss must look like a terrible abrogation of personal responsibility for one's life. Releasement, as described here, might seem to be a recipe for co-dependency, being a "loser," or willingly becoming a doormat. Defenders of authenticity assume that it is only by taking control of your own life that you will be successful and live abundantly. After all, they ask, if I don't take charge of my own life, who will take care of me?

From the standpoint of the ideal of self-loss, in contrast, the project of achieving authenticity seems to have its own problems. For many people, the quest for authenticity has turned out to be a setup for disappointment and failure. Those who are unable to achieve all the goods promised by the culture of authenticity begin to feel that they "must not be doing it right." The demand placed on the seeker of authenticity is quite stringent in many ways. It calls for constant self-surveillance aimed at finding out exactly what one wants and how one feels about things. There is a demand for total transparency of self to self. Yet this self-knowledge has nothing to go on besides what is lit up in the flickering light of self-reflection: the feelings, desires and perceptions rushing by within one's field of consciousness, where there are no markers to indicate whether what shows up is important or peripheral.

Because the project of getting in touch with the true self can prove elusive, a number of large-scale programs have been introduced to show people how to be themselves. More often than not, however, these training programs turn out to be "deceitful, coercive, manipulative, focused on controlling participants, and financially exploitive."[10] Ironically, programs that are designed to help people get in touch with their true selves, supposedly motivated by emancipatory ideals, often have the effect of pressuring people into thinking in ways that confirm the ideology of the founders of the program. As a result, many of those who start out thinking their lives are empty or directionless end up either lost in the mindset of a particular program or feeling they are "never good enough" no matter what they do.

The core assumptions underlying the ideal of authenticity are deeply engrained in our inherited common sense. A little reflection suggests, however, that it is not always clear what the notion of authenticity means or implies. We might ask, for example, What exactly is this "inner self" we are supposed to be true to? What does it include and what does it exclude? What if it turns out that this true self includes some fairly nasty – or, even worse, banal – characteristics, traits we would prefer not to think of as really us? What if many of our deepest and most personal thoughts and desires are actually products of the latest fads and fancies purveyed by the media? And how are we to know that what we find deep within ourselves is something to be embraced and expressed in public space rather than something to be worked over, concealed or replaced? What if the whole notion of the innermost self is suspect? What if it turns out that the conception of inwardness presupposed by the authenticity culture, far from being some elemental feature of the human condition, is in fact a product of social and historical conditions that need to be called into question? Finally, what if the entire project of becoming authentic tends to aggravate the difficulties of living we face in the modern world rather than alleviating or curing them? In other words, suppose it turns out that the ideal of authenticity is more a cause of the problems of living endemic to modern life than it is a way of escaping them!

To address these questions, I want to return to a project Lionel Trilling undertook in his 1971 book, *Sincerity and Authenticity*. This is the task of examining some of the ways people have thought about authenticity at different times, and showing how puzzles about these views led to changes in how people thought about themselves. The guiding question of my inquiry is, How did we get to where we are today and where can we go from here? Following Trilling's lead, I will look at some especially powerful formulations of the ideal of authenticity or its correlates as they appear in literature, religious expression, psychotherapy theory and philosophy. My concern is to understand what such formulations imply and to see whether they contain insights we can learn from today. Like Trilling, I do not have an "answer" to the question for which the notion of authenticity is supposed to provide an answer, the question, How are we to achieve the most fulfilling and satisfying life possible? But I trust that in the course of the journey through different conceptions of how to answer that question, we will gain a deeper understanding of what insights such an answer might embrace and what dangers it should avoid. If we end up knowing something about how some of the great minds of the past have thought about these questions, the journey will have been worthwhile.

Two

We saw that the idea of authenticity presupposes a conception of a true self lying within the individual, a self that contains resources of understanding and purpose that are worth accessing and raising to expression. As we shall see in the next chapter, Lionel Trilling argues in *Sincerity and Authenticity* that the notion of authenticity so understood was not really possible in Western culture until a particular set of ideas had attained currency, and that those ideas did not reach their mature form until the later half of the eighteenth century. Chief among those background ideas is the sharp distinction between *inner* and *outer* that enables us to think of the true self as something that lies within while the false self is something outer. Trilling's claim is that this distinction, with all its ramifications, was not formulated in Western culture until a little over two hundred years ago.

Right away a couple of objections to this claim might spring to mind. Did not Socrates, more than four hundred years before the Christian era, presuppose such a distinction when he invoked the dictum found at the Temple at Delphi, "Know thyself"? And is there not a clear distinction between the inner and the outer running through St. Augustine's *Confessions*? Trilling's point, however, is that our distinctively modern conception of the self – the conception in which the idea of authenticity makes sense – presupposes a much more radical distinction between inner and outer than is found in either of these earlier thinkers.

What exactly did Socrates mean when he said "Know thyself?" There is plenty of room for scholarly debate about this, and some excellent books have appeared suggesting subtle interpretations of the Socratic way of life.[1] One thing seems clear, however, and that is that Socrates probably did not mean what we mean when we think of self-knowledge as a matter of turning inward in order to get clear about our ownmost personal feelings and desires. For it does not seem that Socrates thought of human beings as we do, as self-encapsulated individuals with their own inner, personal being, and with no defining or ineliminable relations to anything outside themselves. According to the Platonic reading of Socrates, humans are regarded as parts of a wider cosmic totality, placeholders in a cosmic web of relations in which what anything is – its *being* as an entity of a particular sort – is determined by its place and function within that wider whole. On this view, the all-encompassing cosmic context embodies a set of ordering principles – an order of "ideas" – that determine both the reality of things and their value relative to the whole. To know yourself, then, is to know above all what your *place* is in the scheme of things – what you are and what you should be as that has been laid out in advance by the cosmic order. Only because finding your place in the scheme of things is what is truly important does it become worthwhile to assess your personal nature to see what idiosyncrasies and personal desires you might have. But note that here personal desires and feelings, far from constituting your true being as a person, are regarded as negative traits – personal liabilities keeping you from measuring up to the ideal type that defines your function as an instance of humankind.

Self-knowledge is therefore a first step not toward "being yourself" as we understand it, but toward a project of excising what is particular and distinctive in yourself in order to be better able to match the ideal that determines your function. That is why, when formulating his conception of justice or ideal harmony in the *Republic*, Plato has Socrates speak of the "origin and pattern of [of the idea of] justice" as "the principle that it is right for someone who is by nature a shoemaker to make shoes and nothing else, for the carpenter to practice carpentry, and the same for the others ..." (443b–c).[2] Just as the right way to be a carpenter is defined by the nature of carpentry as this fits into the overall practices and background of life of the world as a whole, so what is right and good for the individual is defined by the standards that determine in advance the right and proper way to be human in the cosmic order. We might say that the Socratic view is *cosmocentric* in the sense that the cosmos itself determines what things are and how things ought to be. It is for this reason that failing to comply with the cosmic order is seen as something bad. So in the *Laws* we find Plato's criticism of self-centeredness: "you do not seem to be aware that this and every other creation is for the sake of the whole, and in order that the life of the whole may be blessed; and that you are created for the sake of the whole, and not the whole for the sake of you" (903c).[3]

The picture in St. Augustine's *Confessions* is different in many ways. The growing emphasis on inwardness in Christianity had expanded the possibilities for reflection on the inner self and the importance of that practice for living a good life. Augustine's sustained history of his personal inner life makes the *Confessions* deserve, as much as any book for which the claim has been made, the title of "the first modern work."[4]

His long confession, addressed to God, traces his path from his wild and wicked youth through his conversion experience in the garden in Milan to his current state of regeneration and fulfillment. What makes Augustine's work modern is the way it internalizes the narrative structure underlying the Bible as a whole. It finds inner correlates for the biblical notions of beginning, fall, world-defining moment of transformation and salvation, and presents an individual's life as having a narrative structure organized around the idea of salvation. This Christian *soteriological* story-line, in which all events are organized and given meaning in relation to the concern with salvation, provides the narrative schema that continues to shape almost all our self-narratives to this day.

Despite these modern features, however, Augustine's *Confessions* presupposes a different conception of the self than the one underlying our modern conception of authenticity. Certainly there is here the duality of outer "false" self and inner "true" self. But the inner true self is not yet the bounded, self-encapsulated self of modernity. That this is so is evident from the opening words of the *Confessions*, where Augustine says to God, "You have made us toward You" (the expression is equally odd in Latin: *fecisti nos ad te*), where this suggests that the self in its very being is initially, essentially and inextricably bound to God. We are made *toward* God, that is, our proper orientation in life is to be God-directed, and so we are only properly and fully human when we are bound to God as we are always meant to be. Even though our proper direction is God, however, it is generally the case that our sensual desires and worldly preoccupations turn us away from God, with the result that we focus ourselves on worldly affairs and strive to satisfy sensual cravings. We are, for much of our lives, fallen, dispersed, torn apart, out of touch with our true being. The inner quest undertaken in the *Confessions* therefore aims at reversing this direction of falling into worldly things in order to redirect the self toward its proper orientation: being in the right relation to God.

The direction of movement in Augustine's confessions is clearly inward. "All this I do inside me," Augustine says; it is in the inner memory "I meet myself – I recall myself."[5] Or, as he says elsewhere, "Do not go outward; return within yourself. In the inward man dwells truth."[6] But it should be evident that the project of inward-turning in Augustine has as its objective not so much getting in touch with one's own inner self as enabling one to give oneself over totally to God. What constitutes self-realization on this view is what would look like total self-loss to most moderns: release from the ego and acceptance of one's dependence on the source of one's being. Augustine does not even see the self as a unified, self-subsistent source of agency in the way we do. A distinction is made between what *appears* to be the source of our actions – our own will – and what is truly the source of our actions – the First Cause that moves all things. Our actions are often caused by a hidden source: God's will. So Augustine can say to God: "You . . . were then acting in me by the hidden secret of Your Providence" (v. vi); "You brought it about through me, and without my being aware of it" (VI. vii); and, "there is something of man that the spirit of man that is in him does not know" (x. v).[7] Seen in such a light, the entire notion of the self as a unified, masterful, self-contained center of experience and action is called in question. What Augustine finds through his self-inspection is that the self is like a free radical, incomplete and hopelessly unstable unless it is bound in the right way to God.

The trajectory of Augustine's quest is therefore not just inward, not just a matter of self-discovery as we would think of it. Rather, it is "inward and upward."[8] We turn inward only as a means to making contact with and relating ourselves to the Being through whom we first come to be and at any time are. Where Socrates' vision of reality was cosmocentric, Augustine's is *theocentric*. The center of the universe, the standard and measure for what is and what should be, and the very core of our own being as creatures, is the Divine Creator. It follows from this that we only realize our humanity and become what we truly are when we achieve "at-one-ment" with God.

It has become standard practice to distinguish *premodern* ways of thinking and understanding things from the peculiarly *modern* worldview that came to a head in Europe in the sixteenth and seventeenth centuries. In terms of this distinction, Socrates and Augustine, despite their enduring influence and their ability to speak to us across the ages, are premodern thinkers. One way to grasp the difference between modern and premodern is to see that premodern outlooks are not so far removed from the very early and primordial form of experience the French anthropologist Lévy-Bruhl called "participation mystique." For traditional or premodern peoples, experience is shot through with a sense that all things are connected by an underlying life force or principle of being, a force that has been called in different cultures by names such as *mana* or *wakan* or *dharma*. As Owen Barfield describes it, " 'Mana' or 'wakan' (which *we* can only translate by abstract terms like 'totemic principle,' 'life principle,' or – since it is present also in inanimate objects – 'being') is anterior to the individuality of persons and objects; these ... are rather apprehended by [the early premodern] as 'stopping-places of mana.' " In this experience of things, "The human soul [is] one of the "stopping-places" for *mana*, but what differentiates [the premodern] mind from ours is, that it conceives itself to be only *one* of those stopping-places and not necessarily the most significant."[9]

In distinctively premodern societies, then, human beings experience themselves as placeholders in a wider totality, a greater context of life in which many events occur as the result of intentions and purposes that, though inscrutable at times, are not totally unlike our own. "The essence of *original* participation is that there stands behind the phenomena, *and on the other side of them from me*, a represented which is of the same nature as me. Whether it is called 'mana,' or by the names of many gods and demons, or God the Father, or the spirit world, it is of the same nature as the perceiving self, inasmuch as it is not mechanical or accidental, but psychic and voluntary."[10]

Given such an outlook, the boundaries of the self are experienced as more fluid or porous than are ours today. On this older view, my identity as a person is experienced as bound up with the greater context of being in which I am embedded. The self is experienced as what sociologists call an *extended self*: my identity is tied into the wider context of the world, with the specific gods and spirits that inhabit that world, with my tribe, kinship system and family, and with those who have come before and those who are yet to come. Such an experience of the self carries with it a strong sense of *belongingness*, a feeling that one is part of a larger whole. We can see this experience of belongingness in ancient Greek society, where belonging to a household (*oikos*), even in the lowest position, was considered to be so important that a slave in a household was seen as better off than a "free man" (*thēs*), that is, a person who sold his labor on the market and did not belong to any household.[11]

The conception of the self as inextricably tied to a wider context also makes possible the ancient virtue of *reverence*, a way of experiencing things that includes an awareness of the intricate interwovenness of all reality, the dependence of each person on something greater than him- or herself, the consequent sense of human limitations that comes from such an awareness, and an experience of awe before the forces that lie outside human control.[12]

In this experience of the world as an interlocking whole, the understanding of the distinction between the inner and outer is more like a difference of perspectives on one realm of being than it is like an idea of two distinct, fundamentally different realms of being. Moreover, earlier peoples experienced the supernatural as permeating nature, suffusing all things, whereas nature itself is "by nature" supernatural, moved by forces that inhabit things and make them act according to often mysterious intentions. The world seen in this way is a field of meanings in which each thing is an item in the natural order, but is also something more, namely, a sign that signifies other things across a web of meanings. In this sense, the world can be seen by literate people as like a book, a *liber naturae*, in that everything is a sign embodying meaning. These meanings are generally thought of as reflecting the master plan of a divine creator or set of creators. But even the gods are often seen as constrained by a powerful force of fate or destiny – the force of *moira* or *mana* – that surpasses all individuating principles. Nietzsche alluded to such a force when he spoke of the Greek experience of the *Dionysian*, an experience in which the "veil of Maya (illusion)" is torn apart and one encounters "the mysterious Primordial Oneness" that is there prior to the *principium individuationis* and the distinction of manifold things in the world.[13]

Max Weber captured this premodern experience of things in a phrase so catchy it has become something of a cliché. Premodern peoples, he said, lived in an "enchanted garden," a magical place where all things contain hidden powers and where mysterious forces are at work for good and ill. The forces and meanings at work in things generate an underlying order in the world. "Above all," Mircea Eliade writes, "the world . . . has a structure; it is not a chaos but a cosmos, hence it presents itself as creation, as the work of the gods. . . . The cosmic rhythms manifest order, harmony, permanence, fecundity. The cosmos as a whole is an organism at once *real, living,* and *sacred.*"[14] This last sentence is perhaps the most important: the cosmos is very much like a living organism. It has had a birth, it is unfolding, it has its periods of health and sickness, cycles and natural rhythms, and someday it will pass away. All the things that make it up are essential organs in the entire organism; each type of thing has a proper function and role in the healthy unfolding of the totality. And, of course, humans too have their place and their role to play. Just as our body is healthy only so long as each organ is performing its function, so the cosmos as a totality is healthy only so long as humans are living according to the underlying plan for the whole.

Where humans are regarded as parts of a greater living whole, with their own predefined place and their own contribution to make, it is natural to suppose that they have an obligation to achieve for themselves the degree of health and proper functioning needed for the health of the whole. Premodern societies tend to think that there is a proper way to be human that is laid out in the scheme of things itself, prior to and independent of human conventions or preferences. On such a view, one can always distinguish between *what one is* at any given moment – one's actual condition – and *what one ought to be if one were to fully realize one's potential* as a functioning component of the whole – one's purpose (*telos*) in the cosmos. Such an outlook therefore presupposes a conception of life as an ongoing quest aimed at improving the self in order to raise it to the ideal standard dictated by the natural order.

The idea that we have an obligation to shape ourselves in order to measure up to an external criterion is evident in the premodern attitude toward feelings. For this older outlook, what is important is not how you feel at any moment, but rather that you cultivate your feelings so that you will come to feel the right way about the right sorts of things at the right time. Feelings are not givens we have to deal with. They are raw materials we have to work over and discipline in order to make them properly functioning components of a self that is itself a properly functioning component of something greater than itself. In comparison with this older view of feelings, the glorification of feelings that comes on the scene in modern times is just one more step on the path of what C. S. Lewis calls "that great movement of internalization, and the consequent aggrandizement of man and desiccation of the outer universe, in which the psychological history of the West has so largely consisted."[15]

Later in this book we will see that different ways of articulating your life story provide different ways of finding meaning and coherence in the course of events that make up your life. Two different conceptions of lived time, and so two distinctive ways of narrating the course of events that make up a life, can be identified in the thought of premodern peoples. For the earliest premoderns, time is experienced as cyclical, a pattern determined by the natural rhythms of days, works and seasons as they return time and again, year after year. There is a time for planting and a time for harvesting, a time for work and a time for rest, a time for the market and a time when nothing much happens. Here, the flow of life is punctuated by festivals and sacred events, times when people experience a return to the sacred moments of their origins. Mircea Eliade again:

> With each periodical festival, the participants find the same sacred time – the same that had been manifested in the festival of the previous year or in the festival of a century earlier; it is the time that was created and sanctified by the gods at the period of their *gesta* [gestation], of which the festival is precisely a reactualization. In other words the participants in the festival meet in it *the first appearance of sacred time*, as it appeared *ab origine, in illo tempore* [at the origin, in that time].[16]

In this way of experiencing time, there is "a sort of mythical present that is periodically reintegrated by means of rites," so that the possibility of a return to origins is always possible. This cyclical experience of time is powerfully evoked in the African novelist Chinua Achebe's description of life in precolonial Africa:

> The land of the living was not far removed from the domain of the ancestors. There was coming and going between them, especially at festivals and also when an old man died, because an old man was very close to the ancestors. A man's life from birth to death was a series of transition rites which brought him nearer and nearer to his ancestors.[17]

The experience of life as a series of rites carrying a person back to his or her origin makes manifest the sense of belongingness and place characteristic of this older way of seeing things.

The biblical sense of time that comes from early Judaism and Christianity provides an alternative to the cyclical time of premodern peoples. Biblical time tends to be linear – it has a beginning, an unfolding development, and the assurance of an ending – and so it has the sort of narrative structure that is most familiar to us. The course of events is seen as having an author, God, who laid it all out in advance and is able to intervene in the course of events at crucial moments. The idea of a divine source makes it possible to distinguish the epi-sodic and often repetitive sequence of events from the hidden story that is unfolding beneath the surface – the realization of God's will on earth. The biblical conception brings to prom-inence the idea of unique, world-defining events that occur in "the twinkling of an eye," that is, in abrupt, crucial instants that make an absolute difference in world history – events such as the act of Creation, the Covenant, the Advent of Christ, or the End of Times. Finally, biblical time, at least in its Christian form, tends to be symmetrical. Time begins with a peaceable Garden where there is happiness, security and abundance, and it ends when the heavenly city reinstates the conditions of Eden in "paradise" (a word taken from the Greek, *paradeisos*, referring to the walled-in gardens of Persia).

Biblical time starts out from an *archē*, an initiating principle and source that is pregnant with potential and promise, and it ends in a *telos*, the goal of the entire unfolding of events. Such a conception of time, reflecting as it does the temporal struc-ture of the history of salvation, ensures that the course of events has continuity and a point. "The past points to the first things, the future to the last things, and the present to a central presence which connects the past with the future through teleological succession."[18] This conception of time is therefore linear, extending from past to present to future. But, in another sense it is also cyclical, for its end is its beginning, its fulfillment is its promise. The pattern of Christian history is, as Karl Löwith says, "one great detour to reach in the end the beginning."[19]

It would be absurd to glorify the premodern form of experience as if it were some sort of idyllic state. From the standpoint of our modern technological advances and scientific reasoning, it must look like an abyss of dark confusion and superstition. But it is worth noting that, given such an outlook, it was possible to have a fairly strong sense of life's meaning – an ability to feel oneself to be part of some overarching scheme of things that ultimately (if not evidently at any particular moment) made sense. In such a worldview, you just *are* what you *do*. A person just is what he or she does in performing socially established roles and carrying out the functions necessary to the smooth functioning of the wider context of the world. There is no way to draw a sharp distinction between an inner "real me" and what is seen as merely external show. And so there is no basis for formulating a conception of "authenticity" as we understand that notion today. In the enchanted world of earlier times, you are living well if you properly perform the duties assigned to your station in life. One of the highest goals people strive for is honor, where this means being recognized by others as having acted in an estimable way. Exceptional individuals – the heroes and saints – are admired and respected. But for most people, having a place in the shared world and fulfilling one's responsibilities is sufficient to provide a secure sense that one is faring well and achieving one's proper purpose in the scheme of things.[20]

Three

It is a tradition in some twelve-step programs in America to give people celebrating anniversaries a medallion inscribed with the words, "To thine own self be true." I have heard it said that this well-known line from *Hamlet* embodies the entire recovery program, and that nothing is more important than being true to oneself. Whether this is true or not, there can be no doubt that the words "To thine own self be true" speak to us across the centuries in an especially evocative way.

What is less clear is whether those who resonate to this line fully grasp the meaning it had in Shakespeare's play. The words are spoken by Polonius, a sort of comic figure in *Hamlet*, though it seems evident that even in his mouth these particular words should be taken seriously. More interesting is the fact that, when we look at the full context in which the words appear, we find that what is being enjoined is not our current ideal of authenticity, but rather something else. *We* tend to think of authenticity as an end in itself – as something worth pursuing for its own sake. When we look at Polonius' words, however, we see that he is thinking of being true to yourself not as an end in itself, but as a means to some other end. "This above all: to thine own self be true," he says, "And it doth follow, as the night the day, / Thou canst not then be false to any man." What the injunction tells us is that we should be true to ourselves in order thereby to be true to others; there is no suggestion that being true to oneself is valuable in its own right. It seems, then, that what is at stake here is not yet authenticity as we now understand it, but rather the virtue of *sincerity*.[1] It is a social virtue that is at issue here, not a personal virtue of the sort we now take authenticity to be. Nearly two centuries will pass after the composition of *Hamlet* before the idea of authenticity as such will become a pressing concern for large numbers of people.

But even if the ideal of authenticity has not yet taken its contemporary shape in Shakespeare's time, the crucial concepts that will make it possible are beginning to fall into place. Writing around 1590, Shakespeare was on the cusp of a cultural revolution in Europe that was to completely change Western civilization's understanding of the world and the place of humans in it. From the sixteenth to the eighteenth century, Western Europe underwent a transition that led to the formation of what we today call the modern worldview. It is only by gaining some insight into the nature of this distinctively modern cultural outlook that we can see the scaffolding of ideas that made the ideal of authenticity possible.

The sixteenth century has been called a period of crisis in early modern Europe, and it was indeed a crisis in the sense that tensions created by a number of crucial events in Europe rapidly came to a head, culminating in radical transformations in Western civilization.[2] There were sudden and inexplicable shifts in population as the plague waned for the first time in years. Villages swelled with more people than there were roles to fill, and people began to leave their homes and gravitate toward the cities. Together with this movement toward urbanization came the first great mass states, the New

Monarchies. The discovery of the New World led to a sudden influx of wealth into the capitals of Europe, and that in turn led to inflation and economic turmoil of a sort that was totally incomprehensible in terms of older ways of thinking. The Renaissance recovery of ancient texts (saved for centuries by Arab scholars) increased the number of ancient authors available for study. As feudal guild systems broke down, new entrepreneurs accumulated great wealth and created new social classes. Merchants and entrepreneurs were beginning to devise systems of double-entry bookkeeping and were capitalizing voyages and inventions, paving the way for capitalism. There was widespread mobility, both social and geographical, as well as great technological advances as the predecessors of modern scientists, the magi, turned their attention to alchemy, astronomy and the development of automata.

Three crucial events contributed to the formation of the modern worldview. The first was the development of a new form of Christian religious sensibility in Europe, a product of the teachings of successive waves of reformers extending from Jan Hus in Prague to Martin Luther in Wittenberg. Luther's own protest, launched in 1517, led to a shift in emphasis in the understanding of what is involved in the religious life. Protesting against the sale of indulgences in Germany, Luther formulated the central tenet of this new spiritual orientation: "It is not by works but by faith alone that man is saved." What this means is that salvation depends not on external acts in the world (such as buying indulgences or participating in rituals), but rather on the inner condition of the soul in relation to God. If one is to avoid damnation, Luther maintains, one must look inward and cultivate an intense devotion to God. The sole issue for this reformist spirituality becomes the inner state of the individual; the things you accomplish in this world are ultimately irrelevant to the single most important concern in your life – the fate of your immortal soul.

The reformer's emphasis on personal salvation and inwardness leads to what is called *religious individualism*, the absolute centering of the question of religious life on the individual. What is all-important now is the individual's one-to-one relation to God. Luther rejects the Church hierarchy, the practice of confessing one's sins to a priest, and every form of worldly intermediary standing between the self and God. For the sinner, this means that redemption requires a sincere act of contrition and genuine repentance undertaken in one's innermost heart.

The Protestant reforms underway in northern Europe put pressure on the Roman Church to reform itself, leading to what is known as the Catholic Counter-Reformation. Among these reforms was the Church's attempt to standardize methods of confession so that "examining one's conscience" is given a central place. In the practice of confession, the focus is on the individual's intentions rather than on his or her actions; "lust in the heart" is as bad as, and sometimes worse than, a person's actual actions. As a result of these shifts, people in the West more and more become what the French philosopher Michel Foucault has called "subjects of inwardness."[3] Increasingly, people are preoccupied with what is going on inside themselves – their feelings, intentions, desires and motives. And they are able to make a sharp distinction between what is truly them – that is, their individual souls, the seats of their deepest feelings, desires and intentions – and what is only extraneous and transient – their concrete, embodied presence in the world. The distinction between true inner self and outward, bodily existence makes it possible to look on one's body, feelings and needs as things "out there," distinct from oneself, to be worked over according to the demands of faith. With this distinction there also comes an ability to *disown* one's actions, seeing one's worldly involvements as not essential to who one is.

The transformed Christian outlook encourages all people to "wear the world like a loose cloak." The world we find around us, the material world, is seen as a testing ground through which we must pass in order to reach our true home, the spiritual world beyond. We should never let the affairs of this world concern us too much, for the only issue that really matters for us is our immortal soul and its eternal life. Such a view of things carries with it a stance of "contempt for the world," a *contemptus mundi* that goes hand in hand with a rejection of the "pagan" belief that nature has some sort of sacred or supernatural dimension. It is not surprising, then, that many religious thinkers were quick to give their whole-hearted support to the newly appearing science with its mechanized world picture. For the form of Christian belief that helped shape the modern worldview, the idea that we *belong* in any sense to this world begins to look depraved, a vestige of paganism that needs to be uprooted. Certainly, as God's creation, the world and everything in it is good. But this goodness inheres not in the things of the world so much as in the Creator whose glory they manifest.

A second crucial event in the emergence of the modern worldview was the rise of modern science. What makes an early scientist like Galileo so impressive is not just the discoveries he makes, but his ability to see all reality as a *universe*, that is, as a vast, homogeneous aggregate of material objects in contingent causal interactions. Seen from this standpoint, the idea that reality constitutes a meaningful order expressing a divine plan no longer makes any sense. There are no proper functions for things, only ways that things have come to occupy a niche in interactive causal systems. And there is no "proper place" for things, no pregiven *telos* that determines that all things are contributing to the realization of a providential plan. The world is, as the sociologist Max Weber says, "disenchanted": the universe is conceived as a collection of objects in efficient, push–pull causal interactions, with no mysterious or supernatural principles at work anywhere.

Correlated with this conception of what we can know about reality is a transformed understanding of the self who has such knowledge. The objectified and mechanized view of things can arise only for a knowing subject who has stripped off all prejudices and comfortable illusions inherited from the past and is able to adopt a detached, impartial, dispassionate view of things. Scientific mastery of the world requires that we adopt a stance in which we are disengaged subjects, methodical and objective observers who are collecting data and formulating theories. Theory formation itself requires a particular form of abstraction. According to the standard view of scientific method, one starts with the phenomena given in observation and then abstracts out all subject-relative properties of things – the properties things have only in relation to our forms of experience, such as beauty, usefulness, goodness, color, felt heat, smell – in order to isolate the properties that are essential to the thing as it is in itself – namely, the features of a thing that can be quantified, such as mass, velocity, and position. Only those properties of things that are quantifiable are regarded as really in the things.

Underlying the newly emerging science is a fundamental assumption that mathematical idealization reveals reality "as it is in itself." So Galileo claims that "the grand book of the universe . . . cannot be understood unless one first learns to comprehend the language and to read the alphabet in which it is composed. It is written in the language of mathematics, and its characters are triangles, circles, and other geometric figures, without which it is humanly impossible to understand a single word of it; without these, one wanders about in a dark labyrinth."[4] Scientific abstraction calls for an ability to bracket or set aside the commonsense views accepted by one's society as well as the age-old certainties one unreflectively absorbs in growing up into the world. And that in turn calls for an ability to suspend all those beliefs, commitments and concerns that traditionally were seen as definitive of the self. The conception of the self that emerges with this ideal of knowledge is, as Charles Taylor suggests, that of a dimensionless point of pure thought and will. The self comes to be seen as a *subject*, a center of experience and action, set over against a world of objects that are to be known and manipulated.[5] Regarded as a subject, the self lacks any defining or essential relations to anything in the world, even to its own body and emotions. For such a self, anything can be objectified, held out at arm's length and treated as a brute object to be modified and transformed to suit our purposes.

The worldview that emerges with the rise of modern science is *anthropocentric* to the extent that it treats the human self – understood as the knowing subject who objectifies, knows and controls – as the center of the universe. In terms of such an anthropocentric view of things, everything that exists can be said to exist only insofar as it is or can be an object – an *ob-jectum*: that which is "thrown over against" a knowing subject. What had been claimed by the sophists in ancient Greece now becomes self-evident truth: "Man is the measure of all things." At the end of this transition what is left is a world consisting of raw materials at our disposal; nature is encountered, in Heidegger's words, as a giant filling station supplying energy for our needs.[6]

A tremendous feeling of excitement accompanies the transformation in thinking wrought by the new science. Where before our goal on earth might have been seen as finding our place in the cosmos or compliance with God's will, the new aim is seen as attaining power and mastery over nature. Descartes writes that our goal is to "make ourselves masters and possessors of nature,"[7] while Francis Bacon states quite simply, "Knowledge is power." For the new scientific outlook, there are no boundaries to human mastery over nature, only temporary obstacles. Humans can remake the world according to a rational plan, and that means that they can remake themselves as they wish.

The third pivotal event that shaped the modern understanding of self and world was the newly emerging sense of society as something man-made, as a product of human decision and contractual arrangements rather than as something natural or preordained. Such a view is in sharp contrast to earlier views, according to which "the universe [has] a single fundamental order, an order structuring both nature and society, so that the distinction which we mark by contrasting the natural and the social cannot as yet be expressed."[8] In opposition to such older views, the new outlook begins to see society as something anti-natural, as a fortuitous product of human agreements, a sort of association entered into in exchange for certain benefits.

When society comes to be seen as the product of a social contract, when it is regarded as something we have opted into, it can be seen as something "other" to the real self. This is why Margaret Thatcher can say, "There is no such thing as society. There are individual men and women and there are families." But societies do not exist.[9] What we call "society" is an aggregate of individual human beings, a thing that is set over against humans, something that has a life of its own, though it is a life that is not really human. The philosopher Hannah Arendt has shown how the modern idea of the social led people to abandon the old belief that one is fully human only in the interactions of public life and to adopt the modern belief that one is truly oneself only when ensconced in private life.[10] Once again, Shakespeare puts into words this experience of social existence as a matter of just enacting parts and playing roles. "All the world's a stage," Jaques says in *As You Like It*, "And all the men and women merely players: / They have their exits and their entrances, / And one man in his time plays many parts."[11] Life in the social arena is a matter of playing games and reciting lines, and public life is a place where we fret and strut our hour upon the stage and then are seen no more. From this standpoint, social existence is regarded as utterly alien to the real issues of life, a space of artificial existence and self-loss in comparison to one's private moments alone or within one's circle of family or friends.

The experience of the social as "other" to one's true self reinforces the radical individualism already emerging on the religious scene. More than ever before, one has a strong sense of one's own *internal space*: one can see oneself as standing outside or above one's own personality as this appears in public life. People see themselves as objects of interest not because they have accomplished something exceptional or witnessed great things, but simply because as individuals they are of consequence. They write *Confessions* that aim not at testifying to faith but at revealing the inner self, and if they are artists, they paint self-portraits – in Rembrandt's case, nearly forty of them. More and more they live in private rooms and sit on chairs rather than on benches. And the new individual "begins to use the word 'self' not as a mere reflexive or intensive, but as an autonomous noun referring, the [Oxford English Dictionary] tells us, to 'that . . . in a person [which] is really and intrinsically he in contradistinction to what is adventitious.' "[12]

This newly defined self naturally makes a sharp distinction between the features that are part of its worldly existence and what it really is deep within. The modern outlook brings to realization a split between the Real Me – the true inner self – and the persona (from the Greek word for "mask") that one puts on for the external world. With this division comes a sharp distinction between the way one appears in public life and what one truly is in one's inner self. "I have that within that passeth show," says Hamlet, bringing to light an awareness of the gap between one's outer avowals and one's inner intentions.

It is because of this split between inner and outer that the issue of sincerity becomes pressing in the seventeenth and early eighteenth centuries. If the social realm is inherently inhuman, the way to humanize it is to be sincere in our dealings with others: we need to say what we mean and mean what we say. And the best way to be sincere, as we saw earlier, is to follow Polonius' advice and be true to ourselves. If you are true to yourself, you cannot then be false to any man. Not until later will being true to oneself be seen as worthy in its own right, though the pieces needed for such an ideal are already on the table.

*

Especially vivid images of the distinctively modern outlook can be found in the work of Shakespeare's contemporary, Christopher Marlowe. Born in Canterbury in 1564, the year of Shakespeare's birth, Marlowe studied at Cambridge University, received his master's degree in 1587, was arrested for atheism in 1593 and, before his case could be heard, died in a barroom brawl at the age of twenty-nine. Of all the plays written in his short life, none has been more influential than *Doctor Faustus*, the story of a man who in many ways exemplifies the new sort of individual then appearing in Europe. Faustus is a model of the social mobility of the time. "Born of parents base in stock," he nevertheless casts off the sanctions and norms of medieval society and, through his own drive and personal ambition, receives the degree of doctor, ending up with great wealth and power. In many ways, Faustus is a genuinely modern figure. Like the early scientists of the time, he embodies the virtues of courage, fortitude, drive, intellect and constancy. In him we can detect glimmerings of the guiding ideal of the Enlightenment, an ideal Kant formulated two hundred years later in a simple slogan: *Aude sapere*, "Dare to know!"

In his quest for knowledge, power and worldly pleasures, Faustus is contemptuous of the idea of any limits. He calls up the devil Mephostophilis and sells his soul to Satan in exchange for twenty years of sumptuous living in which he can satisfy every desire. The contract stipulates that at the end of that period he will hand himself over to Satan and eternal damnation. The action of the play fast-forwards through those twenty years, highlighting some of Faustus' adventures and achievements, before zooming in on his end.

Written on the cusp of the transition from premodern to modern, *Doctor Faustus* takes place in an enchanted world still suffused with demons and magical forces. There are flashy displays of fireworks, magic tricks, madcap stunts and sudden appearances out of trapdoors to thrill the audience. What is distinctively modern about the play, however, is the way in which the dramatic action takes place not so much in the events on the stage as within the mind and soul of Faustus himself. There is a subjectivizing and interiorization of the dramatic action that sets the play apart from earlier theater. The debates between good angels and bad angels, the ominous sayings of the Old Man, and the parodies of Faustus' actions among the clown figures all seem to reflect and manifest the essentially *inner* turmoil occurring within Faustus' soul.

At the outset of the play, Faustus' monologue imparts a sense of the thrill and exhilaration accompanying the Renaissance quest for knowledge and power. Bored with the medieval three-part course of study – the *trivium* of logic, grammar and rhetoric – Faustus is impatient with the demands of traditional callings such as jurisprudence, medicine and theology. What delights his mind is the prospect of using magic to achieve God's powers:

> O, what a world of profit and delight,
> Of power, of honor, and omnipotence
> Is promised to the studious artisan!
>
> . . .
>
> A sound magician is a demi-god!
> Here tire my brains to get a deity!
>
> (I. i. 51–60)[13]

Surely a chill must have passed through the audience on hearing these words. For there is expressed here the magus' ambition to beget ("get") God within oneself, that is, to become as

God is. Even today, four hundred years later, we feel both admiration for the greatness of Faustus' ambition and discomfort in the face of his overweening pride. Here is a man who defiantly rejects all limits and feels no reverence for anything beyond himself. "This word 'damnation' terrifies me not," he says, "For I confound hell in Elysium," meaning that he denies hell and, like "the old philosophers," believes only in the happy afterlife of ancient paganism (I. iii. 57–9).

Throughout the play, Faustus uses his Satan-given powers to discover ultimate truths about the workings of the universe. At a moment in history when new discoveries and competing claims about cosmology were creating confusion throughout Europe, Faustus is able to soar above the world and see first-hand the true nature of all things. His overview extends even to the outermost sphere and the Prime Mover: "To find the secrets of astronomy," the Chorus says, Faustus rises to the height of Mount Olympus and, "sitting in a chariot bright," looks out over the planets and stars, "even to the height of *primum mobile*" (III. i. 1–10). And Faustus himself brags that

> within the compass of eight days
> We viewed the face of heaven, of earth, and hell,
> So high our dragons soared into the air
> That looking down the earth appeared to me
> No bigger than my hand in quantity —
> There did we view the kingdom of the world,
> And what might please mine eye I there beheld.
>
> (III. i. 69–75)

Like the new scientists formulating their theories about the universe, Faustus strives to achieve a "God's-eye view" of things, a standpoint from which he can encounter reality as it is in itself, uncolored by the limiting perspectives of our human-all-too-human point of view.

But the thrill surrounding Faustus' project of transcendence is counterbalanced by a sense of ominous foreboding that such an attempt to be God must lead to a terrible fall. As his time runs out and his contract with Satan comes to term, Faustus is torn apart by a desperate struggle for his soul. Standing before the most important decision facing any human being, the choice between eternal salvation and eternal damnation, he swings back and forth between turning to God and remaining on the path to perdition. In the play it is quite clear that, if he could only make a sincere act of contrition and repent, God in his infinite mercy could and would forgive him his sins and save his soul. But Faustus' wicked ways hold him back from coming into the right relation to God, and he turns instead to thoughts of suicide: "Where are thou, Faustus? Wretch, what hast thou done?" he cries out, "Hell claims his right and with a roaring voice / Says 'Faustus, come, thine hour is almost come!' " (v. i. 54–5). God's grace is always available to one who achieves an inner state of unconditional devotion. But Faustus is racked by an inability to decisively choose God over Satan. One instant he repents, and the next he takes it back:

> Accursed Faustus! Wretch, what hast thou done!
> I do repent, and yet I do despair:
> Hell strives with grace in my breast!
>
> (v. i. 67–70)

His pride too great, his fall into worldly pleasures gone too far, he is unable to rise and wholeheartedly accept his Creator.

As Faustus comes face to face with eternal damnation, we can hear the inexorable ticking of the clock as time moves forward, carrying him to his ultimate destination. In one of the most powerful images of the confrontation with death in all literature, we experience the unrelenting movement of a life course toward its culmination:

> O Faustus!
> Now hast thou but one bare hour to live
> And then thou must be damned perpetually.
> Stand still, you ever moving spheres of Heaven
> That time may cease and midnight never come:
> Fair nature's eye [that is, the sun], rise, rise again and make
> Perpetual day, or let this hour be but a year,
> A month, a week, a natural day —
> That Faustus may repent and save his soul.
> *O lente lente currite noctis equi!*
> The stars move still, time runs, the clock will strike:
> The devil will come, and Faustus must be damned!
>
> (v. ii. 140–51)

O lente lente currite noctis equi: "Run slowly, slowly horses of the night." The words impart a chilling sense of the unfolding of a life course as it moves toward death. The defining issue of life painted here is not of a promised Second Coming where all souls will assemble and the congregation of the True Church will be saved. The issue is rather a solitary, private one: the salvation of the individual soul in a world-defining instant – "thine hour" that has come. Doctor Faustus in certain crucial respects gives us a distinctively modern picture of the issue of life. We are finite beings who face an end that will define the whole of our being once and for all. It is entirely up to us what that life amounts to, what it adds up to in the end. We are the authors of our fate. Moreover, the meaning and value of that life depends not on our outer accomplishments, but solely on the condition of our inner self: the decisions and commitments we make in shaping our own souls as we traverse life's path. The message is plain and clearly modern: You have but one life to live. This is not a rehearsal. The clock is ticking; time runs its course. It is up to you to make something of your life. You have only yourself to turn to.

So there is something characteristically modern about *Faustus*. But at the same time, the play is still very much part of the older, medieval worldview. The moral of the play is familiar: "And what wonders I have done all Germany can witness, yea all the world, for which Faustus hath lost both Germany and the world, yea heaven itself . . ." (v. ii. 48–51). In other words: What benefits it a man to gain the world and lose his soul? What is important is not the accumulation of material possessions, but the fulfillment of one's inner, spiritual being. Written at the turning point of the transition from premodern to modern times, *Doctor Faustus* tells "the story of a Renaissance man who had to pay the medieval price for being one."[14] A century and a half later, with the most wrenching shifts of science already in the past and the foundations for capitalism firmly in place, there would no longer be any particular "price" to be paid for pride or for the unbridled quest for transcendence.

The exhilaration expressed by *Doctor Faustus* points the way to the changes that were to come for Western civilization in the next few centuries. By the end of the eighteenth century, many of the main ideas of the modern worldview were in place. This new outlook brought with it a breathtaking expansion of human possibilities as old barriers of religious prejudice and domination were torn down. Yet, strange to say, at the very time that new possibilities seemed to be opening up everywhere, the sense of what constitutes the aim of life was contracting and shriveling up. To see why this is the case, we need to clarify the conception of the world and the human self that characterizes the modern worldview.

The modern scientific outlook brought with it a conception of the world that is quite different from the view characteristic of premodern societies. Whereas the traditional worldview sees the world as a meaningful and value-filled *cosmos*, the sort of "enchanted garden" we examined in Chapter 2, modern science portrays the world as a *universe*, that is, as a vast aggregate of material objects in causal interactions. For the scientific outlook, all events that occur in the world must be seen as consequences of underlying deterministic principles: the laws of nature. Given this way of seeing things, it no longer makes any sense to suppose that there is a Providential aim or divine purpose underlying the course of events. Events occur with necessity insofar as deterministic laws underlie all change, but the scientific laws themselves are contingent in the sense that there is no ultimate reason why they are the way they are. It follows, then, that for the scientific point of view, there can be no prospect of finding meaningfulness or value in the objective order of the universe. The universe is cold, heartless and mute. The seventeenth-century religious philosopher Pascal captures the terror this worldview can induce when he writes, "The eternal silence of these infinite spaces terrifies me."[15]

The modern image of reality as a universe is correlated with a distinctive conception of the human self. In the modern worldview, human beings are thought of as essentially minds – as mental containers in which ideas of various sorts circulate. The primary task of humans is seen as gaining knowledge of the external world. We saw that the project of knowing reality calls for an ability to adopt a disengaged, objective stance toward things. In order to know the world as it really is, I must detach myself from all customs, traditions and authority, and concentrate on methodically collecting data and formulating beliefs. This project of attaining knowledge is generally understood to be a solitary project: it is an undertaking that is carried out within the mind of each individual. Descartes formulates this conception of the self as a knowing subject, a self-encapsulated mental substance or a field of consciousness, that represents reality but is not integrally part of it. For the distinctively modern outlook, the self is experienced as a *nuclear self*, something self-defining and self-contained, rather than as the extended self of earlier times. Understood as a knowing subject, the self is a center of experience, with no definitive relations to anything outside itself.

At the same time, however, and rather paradoxically, modernity also regards the self as part of the natural order of the world. To be human is to be one animal among others, an organism subject to the same forces of nature that affect other living creatures. This somewhat schizoid and conflicted modern picture of the self as both a subject of experience and a natural organism was accompanied by an increasingly desiccated conception of the aim of existence. Gone are the older conceptions of "my station and its duties" and the assurance that you are living well so long as you live according to the demands of a wider context of purpose. Though a number of older ideals still circulate in modern Western culture and continue to exert some appeal, there is no longer any sense of an order of things that provides a compelling reason for adopting one set of projects rather than another. For the modern self, projects and undertakings present themselves as anonymous in the sense that none of them is clearly *mine* as opposed to someone else's. To clear-sightedly see this – to see all roles and lifestyles as arbitrary and contingent – is to be liberated from the illusions that spring from custom and brute authority. It is to see that what my life amounts to is something I decide, and that I take over this decision fully only if I resist the siren call of tradition and convention. The only thing that is necessary to my being master of my own life, given this vision of things, is *freedom* from the illusions, pressures and constraints that push me toward one path rather than another. Modern humanity finds that there is no higher end than freedom, where this is seen as the unrestricted ability to choose whatever one wants.

So the ideal of freedom comes to have a special significance for the modern individual. But, as social critics quickly noted, there seems to be something vacuous about this ideal of freedom: as Philip Rieff says, with this ideal of freedom, modern humanity is put in the painful predicament of being "freed to choose and then having no choice worth making."[16] The conception of freedom as "negative liberty," as freedom *from* constraints, seems to undermine the meaningfulness of freedom altogether. For when every option is seen as equally optional, and when choice is seen as having no basis other than momentary preference or feeling, then it is hard to see how there can be anything like real choice at all. Freedom starts to look like a matter of falling prey to each passing whim, a sort of slavery to one's caprice, rather than meaningful agency.

A little reflection suggests that there is something incoherent about taking freedom as one's highest goal in life. In our actual experience, freedom strikes us as valuable not because it is an end in itself, but because it enables us to pursue and achieve the things we regard as genuinely worth having. The courageous struggle for freedom that made possible modern democracy gained its meaning from the concrete conditions of oppression and domination it fought to overcome. Once freedom has been achieved, however, the quest for freedom no longer makes much sense. This is because freedom is in fact more like a means to accomplishing ends than it is an end in itself. The problem with thinking of freedom as an end in itself becomes apparent when we look at how freedom is treated as the highest goal of life in the writings of existentialist authors. The French existentialist Simone de Beauvoir, for example, imagines freedom as the supreme aim of life and formulates the ideal as follows:

> Every subject plays his part as such specifically through exploits or projects that serve as a mode of transcendence; he achieves liberty only through a continual reaching out toward other liberties. There is no justification for present existence other than its expansion into an indefinitely open future.[17]

This is heady stuff, of course, but it can leave us a bit puzzled. What exactly is de Beauvoir trying to say? The point seems to be that I can affirm myself as a subject only if I freely undertake projects whose goal is the greater expansion of my freedom, and that goal is important because it makes it possible for me to undertake more projects aimed at expanding my freedom, and that is valuable because it enables me to reach out to even greater freedom, and that is good because . . . What? When we try to unpack the language of existentialism, it begins to sound more like an exercise in futility than a path to achieving a meaningful and fulfilling life.

Freedom is essential to our modern image of ourselves as

self-defining subjects. But when it comes to deciding which course of action we should pursue, it does not seem to provide much direction. That may be why the notion of pursuing *happiness* becomes so important in the modern period. Starting in the eighteenth century, and continuing through today, the notion of happiness comes to define the proper aim of life. "You should do what will make you happy." "What is really important is that you are happy with your life."

But what is happiness? What is this ideal state that now serves as the final court of appeals of a well-lived life? In his classic work, *The Pursuit of Happiness*, Howard Mumford Jones traces the transformations that occur in the concept of happiness, this "glittering generality," from the eighteenth-century ideal of serene contentment in the bosom of one's family to the twentieth-century notion of happiness as a pleasurable feeling.[18] Through the course of this development, it becomes increasingly clear that defining happiness in terms of any substantive state of affairs (faith, family, friends, wealth, success, moral fiber, etc.) begs the question about what constitutes the good life and thereby seems to put constraints on our freedom of choice. As a result, happiness today has come to be regarded as a specific sort of feeling – a pleasurable and enduring sense of well-being – no matter what the cause of that feeling might be. Freedom in turn is regarded as the ability to pursue happiness as one sees fit. Happiness and freedom are the privileged goals of living according to the modern outlook.

Though this modern image seems simple and clear-cut, it is not at all evident that it provides a trustworthy guide to how one should live. Social critics have noted, for example, that the pursuit of happiness runs the risk of itself being a source of misery. Consider what the pursuit of happiness involves. We seek happiness, and we do so by trying to satisfy our desires. Each time we satisfy a desire, there is a familiar pleasant feeling of satisfaction. But it is part of the psychology of desire that this feeling of satisfaction tends to pass after a while, with the result that we soon begin to feel new desires. When these new desires themselves have been satisfied, there is a temporary feeling of fulfillment, but this is soon followed by new feelings of emptiness and desire. The result is an endless cycle of desire followed by temporary satisfaction followed by adaptation followed by new desires, a cycle that in the end can lead to compulsive behavior and finally to all-pervasive feelings of emptiness, futility and despair.

A powerful diagnosis of the spiritual sickness that results from modernity's desiccated vision of life's aims is found in Dostoevsky's *The Brothers Karamazov*. According to one of the characters in that novel, when people interpret "freedom as the multiplication and rapid satisfaction of desires," they "distort their own nature, for many senseless and foolish desires and habits and ridiculous fancies are fostered in them. They live only for mutual envy, for luxury and ostentation. . . . And it's no wonder that instead of gaining freedom, they have sunk into slavery."[19] Where the ultimate goal of life is trying to feel good through satisfying every desire, people become addicted to such activities as shopping, possessing fancy toys, fixing up their houses, looking good, and using drugs, alcohol and consumer spirituality to fill the empty place in their souls. Dostoevsky's verdict on such a life is that living with no higher aim than pursuing pleasurable feelings is self-defeating: "For how can a man shake off his habits, what can become of him if he is in such bondage to the habit of satisfying the innumerable desires he has created for himself?"[20]

Already in the eighteenth century, and increasingly in the

nineteenth century, the constellation of ideas that make up the modern world came to be criticized by perceptive social critics. To many it became evident that modernity engenders a way of life characterized by obsessive pursuits that lead to alienation not only from others, but from one's own self as a human being with feelings and needs. While the modern worldview opened doors to previously unimagined possibilities of human activity and self-responsibility, it also tended to undermine the ability to formulate a coherent, viable image of the ends of living. It was in the backlash against the new constellation of ideas shaping the modern mind that our modern concept of authenticity first appeared on the scene.

Four

The new scientific worldview gained increasing hold on the minds of intellectuals and even ordinary people by the beginning of the nineteenth century. For the thinkers of this so-called "radical Enlightenment" outlook, the only thing that exists in the universe is matter in causal interaction. The human mind itself, on this view, is nothing other than the functioning of the brain of an organism that has evolved through various stages and now exhibits behavior that is merely a product of its adaptation to a physical environment. For those who accept this perspective on things, the scientific worldview brings with it a powerful sense of human progress and emancipation. It promises to free us from the old illusions bred by religious dogma, social custom, superstition and tradition. Using scientific method, we can discover the ultimate truth about reality. The Faustian dream reaches its culmination in the assurance that empirical observation and rational theorizing will reveal everything there is to know about reality.

At the same time, the Enlightenment's project of achieving emancipation from all prejudice and illusion tends to undermine the traditional belief that knowledge of nature can provide us with information about how we should live our lives. There is an increasing tendency to suppose that nature is inherently value-free – it just *is* – and that any values are ultimately arbitrary, ungrounded human inventions. Such an assumption is evident in Sigmund Freud's comment that "the moment one inquires about the meaning or value of life one is sick, since objectively neither of them has any existence."[1] For Freud and like-minded moderns, values are found not "out there" in the world of living beings, but rather "in here," in the minds of humans. They are projections of our desires and feelings onto things, human constructions with no correlates in the objective order outside our minds. When it comes to the question of what goals are worth pursuing, then, the best answer that can be given is the utilitarian answer: the goal of life is to increase pleasure and avoid pain. The idea that there could be anything higher at stake in life than promoting pleasant feelings comes to look like one of those old superstitions the triumph of scientific reason was supposed to eliminate.

The critics who challenged the radical Enlightenment outlook were united in the belief that the modern way of seeing things has been purchased at a terrible cost. There is the feeling that, with the coming of the disenchanted outlook of modernity, a primal unity and wholeness in life has been lost. When nature appears as a brute object of sense perception, as something merely on hand to be mastered and controlled, it can no longer speak to us of life-guiding purposes and meanings. The result is that humans find themselves cut off from nature, unable to experience the natural world as their proper home. Even more unnerving, the invidious distinction between reason and feelings leads people to feel torn apart within themselves, torn away from the inner resources that give us a sense of what is truly important. As a result of the divisiveness and fragmentation created by the Enlightenment outlook, life loses the quality of integrity and meaningfulness it was thought to have had in earlier times.

Romanticism, the undercurrent of reaction against Enlightenment rationality and mechanization, developed as a backlash against the fracturing and disruption brought about by the modern worldview. The term "Romanticism" refers to a sprawling and uneven set of tendencies and cultural forms that developed at various times and in very different ways in different parts of Europe in response to the Enlightenment worldview. Even setting dates for the beginning and end of Romanticism is problematic: the precursors of Romanticism were already at work in the late eighteenth century, and the movement is in some ways as alive and potent today as it was in the nineteenth century when it reached its zenith.

Instead of trying to say anything general about Romanticism, I will limit myself to noting three features of the Romantic mind that continue to be important in our contemporary culture of authenticity. The first is the attempt to recover a sense of oneness and wholeness that appears to have been lost with the rise of modernity. The second is the conviction that real "truth" is discovered not by rational reflection and scientific method, but by a total immersion in one's own deepest and most intense feelings. And the third is Romanticism's discovery, at the limits of all experience, that the self is the highest and most all-encompassing of all that is found in reality.

The ideal of recovering a lost sense of wholeness and oneness is central to the novel *Hyperion*, written by one of the most representative of the Romantic poets in Germany, Friedrich Hölderlin. This book, published in two parts in 1797 and 1799, takes the form of a series of letters written by a man from Greece, Hyperion, to a German friend named Bellarmin. Hyperion, who had spent some time abroad traveling in Western Europe and had absorbed some of the forms of life characteristic of the West, discovers on his return to Greece that through his travels he has become cut off from the experience of wholeness he had once known in his ancient homeland.

Hyperion's letters express his nostalgic longing for a lost experience of oneness. He offsets an idealized picture of primal Greek experience against the rationalism and mechanization of Western modernity. The Romantic yearning for simpler, more integrated times appears in two forms in *Hyperion*. The first is an evocation of a primordial state of connectedness with all things, an experience Hyperion recovers for a moment on his return home:

> To be one with all – this is the life divine, this is man's heaven. To be one with all that lives, to return in blessed self-forgetfulness into the All of Nature – this is the pinnacle of thoughts and joys, this the eternal mountain peak, the place of eternal rest.[2]

In the primal wholeness of all that lives, death is no longer; there is only the youthfulness of ever-new being:

> To be one with all that lives! At those words Virtue puts off her wrathful armor . . . and Death vanishes from the confederacy of beings, and eternal indivisibility and eternal youth bless and beautify the world. (Ibid.)

This experience is lost, however, the moment Hyperion engages in reflection:

> On this height I often stand, my Bellarmin! But an instant of reflection hurls me down. I reflect, and I find myself as I was before – alone, with all the griefs of mortality; and my heart's

refuge, the world in its eternal oneness, is gone; Nature
closes her arms, and I stand like an alien before her and
understand her not. (Ibid.)

The second experience of oneness evoked in Hyperion is the
experience of childhood and childlike innocence, prior to the
distancing relations and hardening of experience brought
about by growing up:

Yes, divine is the being of the child, so long as it has not been
dipped in the chameleon colors of men. The child is wholly
what it is, and that is why it is so beautiful. The pressure of
Law and Fate touches it not; only in the child is freedom. In
the child is peace; it has not yet come to be at odds with itself.
(p. 24)

In our earliest childhood years, and in the oneness with nature
characteristic of pre-reflective, pre-rationalizing experience,
we are in touch with a primal truth.

Hyperion's evocation of a lost oneness suggests that we
have been torn away from a vital, dynamic order of life cours-
ing through nature, an order that was known to earlier
experience but is now concealed by the detached stance of
rational knowing and reflective awareness. By recalling the
earlier state, Hyperion conveys the belief that life has depth,
beauty, vibrancy and intensity when it is at its source, but is
brittle and disjointed when it is uprooted from the source.[3]
The Greek letter-writer suggests to his German friend that the
loss of primordial connectedness he experiences results from
the propensity to engage in reasoning and reflective thought
he picked up while living in Germany.

Ah! Had I never gone to your schools! . . . Knowledge has
corrupted everything for me. Among you I became so truly

What is the source? (basis)

> reasonable, learned so thoroughly to distinguish myself from
> what surrounds me, that now I am solitary in the beautiful
> world, an outcast from the garden of Nature in which I grew
> and flowered, drying up under the noonday sun. (p. 23)

It is the nature of rational reflection that it requires a gap between the reflecting "I" and the stream of life from which it is dissociated in reflection and knowing. Because it introduces a fissure into the stream of life, knowing undermines the wholeness of the self. It is because rationality breaks apart consciousness that Hyperion can speak of Enlightenment rationalists as "barbarians who imagine that they are wise because there is no more heart in them" (p. 26).

The story-line in Hyperion is typical of Romantic ways of emplotting events in that it reflects the basic narrative structure of the Bible. As in the biblical story-line, there is a beginning – a state of pure and unspoiled Oneness with life and nature – followed by a Fall – the loss of Oneness that results from reflection and knowledge ("knowledge has corrupted everything for me" (p. 23)). And as in the biblical narrative, there is a dark night of the soul ("the midnight of anguish" (p. 167)), a moment of crisis, and ultimately the prospect of rebirth and salvation.

At the end of Hyperion, Hölderlin expresses in almost hallucinatory images the prospect for a return to Oneness:

> O thou, . . . Nature! . . . Men fall from thee like rotten fruits,
> oh, let them perish, for thus they return to thy root; so may I,
> too, O tree of life, that I may grow green again with thee.
> (p. 169)

What is revealed in this moment of vision is that all that lives is alike: "Ye springs of earth! Ye flowers and ye woods . . . We are free, we are not narrowly alike in outward semblance, [but] in the inmost of our inmost selves we are alike!" The secularized experience of redemption that comes at the end of the novel, like its biblical prototype, involves a return to origins:

> Like lovers' quarrels are the dissonances of the world.
> Reconciliation is there, even in the midst of strife, and all
> things that are parted find one another again in the end, . . .
> all is one eternal glowing life. (p. 170)

It is important to see that the recovery of wholeness pictured by the Romantic imagination is not just a return to an original state, but is a reunification at a higher level, a recovery that, having passed through the painful process of division and reintegration, achieves a higher level of insight than was possible at the outset. It is the return to origins captured by T. S. Eliot in Little Gidding when he writes, "And the end of all our exploring / Will be to arrive where we started / And know the place for the first time."[4] Reunification with nature is achieved not by knowing, but by being fully immersed in the life-process in such a way that the "inmost of our inmost selves" resonates with all that is.

No one in history contributed more to the development of Romanticism, and also to the idea of authenticity, than the French writer and philosopher Jean-Jacques Rousseau. Like many others in the mid-eighteenth century, Rousseau was highly suspicious of everyday social existence. Society is seen as the primary cause of the loss of wholeness and unity characteristic of contemporary life. But Rousseau's indictment of society went even further. In his Discourse on the Origin of Inequality of 1755, he argued that society itself is the cause of most of the miseries and corruption of modern existence. When humans lived in the "state of nature," he suggests, they were free beings, enjoying simple, uncomplicated lives. It is only with the emergence of society, and the mutual dependence, inequality, servitude and oppression it creates, that the deformation of human nature begins.

Many of Rousseau's diagnoses of modern life still ring a bell for us today. Anticipating the self-help gurus of our own time, Rousseau puts forward the view that it is the way we live in modern society that causes our illnesses. "Most of our ills are of our own making," he says; "we could have avoided nearly all of them by preserving the simple, regular and solitary lifestyle prescribed to us by nature."[5] The status relations and demands of social role-playing lead to "excessive idleness among some, excessive labor among others." Consuming overly refined foods leads to indigestion. Modern social existence leads to "staying up until all hours, excesses of all kinds, immoderate outbursts of every passion, bouts of fatigue and mental exhaustion," and innumerable other maladies (p. 22). And it is not just our physical health that is destroyed by modern life. Constant reflection and calculative reason distort our nature and tear us away from the simple understanding of right and wrong we have from birth. "The state of reflection is contrary to nature," Rousseau says; it runs against the grain. In a verdict meant to shock the Enlightenment culture of his day, he concludes that "the man who meditates [that is, engages in thoughtful reflection] is a depraved animal" (p. 22).

In his effort to separate what is original from what is artificial in the present nature of man, Rousseau tries to grasp human beings in their natural state. But he is aware that this is not an easy task, for it demands that we "have a proper understanding of a state which no longer exists, which perhaps never existed, [and] which probably never will exist" (pp. 12–13). The difficulties of this project notwithstanding, Rousseau comes to the conclusion that humans are by nature good. We find this claim expressed forcefully in his study of child-rearing, the novel *Emile*, where he says, "Let us lay it down as an incontrovertible rule that the first impulses of nature are always right; there is no original sin in the human heart, the how and why of the entrance of every vice can be traced [back to social conditions]."[6]

When we turn away from society's complicated rules of propriety and decorum and look into our own hearts, we find that there are two basic, innate principles that guide us in our unspoiled state. First, we see that we are by nature "ardently interested in our well-being and our self-preservation."[7] Such concern with one's own well-being is the good, healthy self-love that makes us care for ourselves: "Self-love is always good, always in accordance with the order of nature;" Rousseau writes, "we must love ourselves above everything."[8] Second, we find an inbuilt principle that "inspires in us a natural repugnance to seeing any sentient being, especially our fellow-man, perish or suffer."[9] This spontaneous pity for the unfortunate keeps us from becoming self-centered monsters.

All natural rules of right flow from these two principles. The child-rearing instructions in *Emile* therefore focus on the need to let the child develop without being affected by the influence of social decorum and conventions. The main thing, Rousseau says, "is that the child shall do nothing because . . . of other people, but only what nature asks of him; then he will never do wrong."[10] We need to listen not to society, but to the voice of nature, a voice that is heard not by listening to the chatter of the public world, but by turning inward and accessing our most spontaneous and basic feelings. "Let us obey the call of nature," Rousseau tells us, "we shall see that her yoke is easy and that when we give heed to her voice we find joy" (p. 301). Though our judgments about the world are derived from the ideas we acquire from outside ourselves, the ultimate criterion of worth of what we discover is given by our innermost feelings: "it is by these feelings alone that we perceive fitness and unfitness of things in relation to ourselves, which leads us to seek or shun these things" (p. 303).

Given the fundamental importance of natural feelings, we can see that the Enlightenment's privileging of reason creates a one-sidedness and disequilibrium within the mind, an imbalance leading ultimately to fragmentation within the self. To heal the division within the self, we must regain our original grasp of the limits of reason. It is not reason that gives us guidance in understanding what is worthwhile; feelings alone show us what genuinely matters.

For Rousseau, our ultimate guide in life should be the voice of conscience: "Conscience! Conscience! Divine instinct, immortal voice from heaven; sure guide for the ignorant and finite indeed, yet intelligent and free; infallible judge of good and evil, making man like God!" (p. 304). Note that in this picture of our situation, our feelings raise us to the level of God. When we act on our feelings, we are doing as God would do. And, in fact, even though Rousseau never denies the existence and grandeur of God, like others in his time he seems to have less room for God in his vision of what guidance humans should have in acting in the world. Where God had stood in the vision of reality of earlier thinkers, Rousseau and his followers place Nature. We are doing the right thing so long as we follow nature, for nature "does everything for the best," and so has placed in us the instincts and feelings that will always lead us in the right direction (p. 52).

Though Rousseau never appears to use any word that could be translated as "authenticity," it seems obvious that all of the core assumptions built into the concept of authenticity are fully worked out in his writings. There is the distrust of society and its demands and the idea of an inner, "true self," where this notion captures both the spontaneous child within and the "noble savage" that existed (or is imagined to have existed) in some "happy age" in the distant past. There is the nostalgia for an earlier state and the intimation that by turning inward and hearing the inner voice of the true self, one might make contact with the great groundswell of Nature from which we have sprung. There is the idea that our access to the source of our being is achieved not by cognitive reflection, but by *feeling*. And there is a conception of freedom as liberation from socially imposed constraints.

Rousseau's writings provide a vision of the human condition that provides a perfect exemplar of what Lionel Trilling had in mind in his definition of "authenticity." What authenticity involves, according to Trilling, is "a wider reference to the universe and man's place in it, and a less acceptant and genial view of the social circumstances of life." With this negative stance toward social existence, "much that was once thought to make up the very fabric of culture has come to seem of little account, mere fantasy or ritual, or downright falsification."[11] In relation to the ideal of authentic existence, the social circumstances of life appear to be matters of game-playing and enacting parts with no real connection to who we are. All these notions are built into Rousseau's conception of what life should be.

We might pause for a moment to note how appealing Rousseau's picture is to us today. Many of us have felt that the social roles, calcified conventions and frenzied busyness of social existence are blocking us from our ability to be all we can be. Like Dr. Phil, we have felt the need to turn away from our social involvements in order to ask ourselves what we really want and need. This inward-turning is motivated not by a self-centered fascination with quirky mental events and states. On the contrary, like Rousseau, many of us assume that gaining access to the inner self will get us in touch with something of profound significance. The innermost self is experienced as a doorway to a context of meaning that is greater than either the social world or the passing psychological occurrences within us. The turn inward is supposed to lead us to a dimension of the self that transcends our particularity. It is deep within myself that I find that I am part of Nature or The World Spirit or Humankind or the realm of imagination, creativity and beauty. This is why Trilling says that the ideal of authenticity embodies a "wider reference to the universe [perhaps *cosmos* is a better word here] and man's place in it." By turning away from the pretence and deception of society, I find the place where I truly belong: my natural home as a spiritual or childlike or creative or quasi-divine being. The trajectory of the project of being authentic is homologous to the Christian quest we examined in Chapter 2: inward and upward. For the Romantic mind most of us still share, turning inward is all about getting in touch with something greater than ourselves, even though this "something greater" is, for many of us, no longer God as traditionally conceived.

The Romantics who followed the path laid out by Rousseau saw all of life as a quest aimed at recovering what was known to pre-socialized noble savages and experienced by us in our early childhood. It would be wrong, however, to suppose that the Romantic quest in its most mature form is simply an attempt to get in touch with an antecedently given order of nature, a natural realm with determinate properties in its own right. The quest starts out as an attempt to recover a lost oneness with nature, but it is not content with achieving oneness with the natural world. On the contrary, for Romantic thinkers, getting in touch with nature is seen as only an initial step on a longer path that leads to an even higher level of insight and realization. For the true goal of the Romantic quest is spiritual autonomy, and in relation to this goal the experience of oneness with nature is merely a preliminary stage. The self must pass through a stage of thinking that it is one with nature and that this is the highest truth, but this is only a transitional stage, a stage that itself will be surpassed as the mind reaches a yet higher truth. The ultimate destination is the recognition of the absolute priority of the creative powers of the human imagination over both the natural self and nature. At the culmination of the Romantic quest, organic energy is superseded by creative energy. Romanticism aims not at humanity's oneness with nature, but at the ultimate humanization of nature in the apotheosis of human creativity.[12]

The Romantic picture of a path leading through nature to something higher is evident in the finished portions of Wordsworth's epic poem, *The Recluse*. In the long autobiographical prelude to this work, called *The Prelude*, Wordsworth evokes the experience of nature he had as a young boy. Nature is understood by him not as it is by us, not as the totality of independently existing natural objects in the world. Instead, nature is a power and a spiritual force, something to behold in awe and reverence, something that is "always a guide leading beyond itself."[13] The poem begins with a premonition of spiritual autonomy, the promise of the coming of a sublime state that surpasses the dependence of sensory experience on nature (p. 290). But before this premonition can be realized, the poetic mind first passes through a dark night of the soul in which it thinks it is distinct from nature. As the poem unfolds, this darkness is dispelled as the poet achieves an emerging sense of oneness of mind with nature. This experience of oneness is not the final resting place, however, for as the poem moves toward its climax, the experience of oneness is itself left behind, and the mind becomes aware that its own imagination is the ultimate source of the meaning and order of nature. In the end, mind itself is the ultimate source and nature turns out to be its product.

In the experience of the dependence of reality on the mind, Wordsworth presupposes an understanding of things that parallels the development of idealism in German philosophers from Kant and Fichte to Hegel and beyond. According to idealism, what we call "reality" is always something that is organized and made intelligible in terms of the forms of perception, understanding, and above all imagination that are already built into the experiencing mind. If this is the case, however, then nature is not something "out there" that the mind somehow encounters and experiences. What the poet discovers is that it is the human mind that forms and generates what presents itself in experience as nature. And if that is the case, then the mind and its productive imagination turn out to play the same role that God played in the premodern worldview. Wordsworth speaks of "that licentious craving in the mind / To act the God among external things, / To bind, on apt suggestion, or unbind."[14] What imparts order by binding and unbinding is neither something in the cosmos itself nor a transcendent creator and source of being. It is the human mind that defines and creates the order of being it encounters.

Wordsworth only discovers this priority of mind over nature slowly in the course of his life's journey. The crucial turning point in the poem occurs when nature manifests itself to the poet as inherently meaningful and value-laden, as a source of guidance and direction for our lives. This is experienced at first as an evocation of the premodern sense of the world as a cosmic order shot through with meanings: "All / That I beheld," Wordsworth says, "respired with inward meaning." It is this experience of nature as meaningful and value-laden that motivates the recognition that it is mind that constitutes nature. The world Wordsworth finds around him is found to speak of meanings and ideals that are invisible to the crass standpoint of calculative reason and scientific perception. But this discovery of meaning in nature is immediately found to be something he has created himself. This is what he means when he says, "I held a world about me; 'twas my own, / I made it; for it only liv'd to me."[15] In other words, nature is found to be something constituted and given meaning by the creative imagination. And this means that it no longer exerts any binding authority on human thought and action: as something we make, it cannot guide us in our making activity.

As if recoiling from the fully anthropocentric implications of this idea, Wordsworth quickly adds that the meaningful world that only lived to him also lived "to the God who look'd into my mind" (III. 146). But note that in this reference, God is merely a vestige of what was meant in earlier beliefs. For the Romantic mind, God is a purely formal placeholder with no real role to play, "an adventitious and nonoperative factor, . . . a purely formal remainder of His former self."[16]

Where traditional religious belief in the West had presupposed a triad of God–Nature–Man and had interpreted the human condition in terms of this three-way set of relations, Romanticism at first replaces the traditional schema with a dyadic structure, Nature–Man, in which the place formerly held by God is usurped by the creative imagination of Man. Eventually, however, even this dyadic structure is displaced. At the highest level of insight, it becomes clear that nature itself, experienced as a context of meaning and purpose, receives its determinate characteristics from the activity of the human mind. And when nature is seen to be a product of the mind, all that is left of the original triad is the monad: Man, or Mind. The ultimate metaphysical reality is the human Self, independent of and untouched by anything outside itself, in its own unbounded freedom creating realities for itself, and in no way answerable to anything outside itself. In Wordsworth's words, "the mind of man becomes / A thousand times more beautiful than the earth / On which he dwells" (XIV. 450–2).[17]

The development of ideas is noteworthy here. The Romantic backlash against the modern desanctification of nature starts out from an intense dissatisfaction with what it sees as the Enlightenment's desiccated picture of the world as a meaningless, value-free aggregate of physical objects. In its effort to retrieve the older sense of nature as an enchanted garden, it undertakes a quest aimed at recovering lost origins. Given the immense power of the modern scientific image of reality, however, it becomes evident that retrieving the natural world in its supernatural significance is to be achieved not by making contact with nature itself. Instead, the enchanted world of earlier times is accessed by turning inward, that is, by hearing the voice of nature that lies within us. Romanticism's "internal spiritual journey in quest of a lost home" seeks ultimate sources within the mind itself.[18]

What is discovered during this journey, however, is that the enchanted garden of olden times is enchanted only because it is created by the mind itself. Nature turns out to be a second-class citizen in the order of the real, something derivative from and dependent upon imagination. And so it appears that, when we arrive at the place where we started "and know the place for the first time," what we know is that this place is something in us, not something out there independent of us. In saying that the enchanted garden is something "in here" and not "out there," it can be argued that Romanticism, far from providing an alternative to scientific objectification, simply turns reality over to the sciences once and for all and rests content with creating its own reality in imagination. Romanticism's final story is that we can let science have reality, because *we* have another reality – a special reality that is in here, within the self. Given this view of things, however, the self is not just the center of the universe. It *is* the universe. For the sort of Romanticism found in *The Prelude*, there is simply no place for anything outside the self.

It should be obvious that a tremendous burden is placed on the idea of the self in the new culture of authenticity that took shape in the nineteenth century. As the self is raised to its status as ultimate reality, the natural question to ask is: What *is* this self? To address this question, I want to follow the Swiss intellectual historian, Jean Starobinski, and take a look at Rousseau's attempt to answer the question, Who am I?[19] Given the centrality of this question to Rousseau and

Rousseau's influence on our thinking, following his path of thought should show us a great deal about how we understand the self today.

The question "Who am I?" is one Rousseau feels he can answer quite directly, for, as he says, "I feel my own heart," *Je sens mon coeur*. That is to say, the self is something we know through a direct self-awareness that relies solely on feeling. There is a direct presence of self to self, immediate access that is given not to cognitive reflection, but to what Rousseau calls the "sentiment of existence." Certainly, feelings are subject to change, but "at each moment [feeling's] authority is absolute; it inaugurates the truth."[20] In the immediacy of self to self in feeling, there is no way to insert a wedge that would make possible questions about the truthfulness of what is presented. Here, self-presence just *is* truth: I truly *am* what I feel myself to be.

So there is a basis for self-knowledge in the direct presence of self to self. But Rousseau does not think that this self-presence is sufficient for the full sort of self-clarification and self-discovery he seeks. When it comes to achieving the deepest kind of self-knowledge, it is not enough simply to be transparent to oneself. One must also be recognized by others for what one is. There is the idea here that you can truly *be* such-and-such a person only if others see you as being that person. The look of the other is needed to confirm and stabilize one's identity. For this reason, Rousseau produces an impressive number of autobiographical writings throughout his life. His most famous work, the *Confessions*, is followed by the autobiographical passages of the *Dialogues*, which in turn are followed by self-examinations of the *Reveries*.

What we find in Rousseau's autobiographical writings is a powerful compulsion to tell all, a compulsion that reflects a conception of human nature that M. H. Abrams calls an *expressive* view and Charles Taylor calls *expressivism*.[21] The expressivist view starts out from the idea that inner experience invariably is driven to externalize itself in a concrete form in the world. Experience, by its very nature, ex-presses itself – it presses itself outward – striving to give itself shape in gestures, language and enduring creations. For Rousseau, the subjective life "is not 'hidden,' not buried in psychological 'depths.' It bubbles spontaneously to the surface" in outpourings of self-revelation aimed at revealing who exactly he is.[22]

Rousseau sees himself as having a special mission in this project of self-expression. On the one hand, he believes that every person embodies the archetype of humanity within himself, so that undistorted self-access can reveal the truth about the natural state of humans to anyone who undertakes it. On the other hand, Rousseau thinks he is in an especially good position to gain insight into the human condition through self-exploration. Coming from a lower-class family, he suggests, he has no status or estate of his own, and so his vision is not biased by any particular perspective. Coming from Geneva and living and writing among the French, he is, in a sense, stateless, and in this respect he is also open to a variety of points of view. Given his circumstances, his self-examination is as unclouded by social interpretations as anyone's can be. It is precisely for this reason that his experience has universal significance (pp. 184–5).

So Rousseau in his writings undertakes one project of self-exploration after another. But these undertakings seem to point up a problem in the very nature of self-discovery. Rousseau never doubts that his life has a unified shape. But he also thinks that the definitive truth of his life can be established only through the process of expressing it in a formulation that is accepted by others. If he *imposes* a unifying form onto the life story, however, the reader will suspect that the picture that emerges is a product of editing and embellishing, and so is not the true picture. Rousseau resolves, therefore, to present all the material of his life in its rawest, unedited form, and leave it to his readers to form their own opinion of who he is. "Everything fits together," he writes, "it is all in my character . . . and this bizarre and singular assemblage requires all the circumstances of my life to be fully unveiled."[23] It is up to the reader to discover the underlying unity in the multiplicity of events.

But Rousseau recognizes that even this ideal of simply presenting the facts is problematic. For, as Starobinski observes, "It is impossible to reconstruct the factual past. Memory is finite as well as fallible. Few scenes are vividly recorded. . . . What is more, my present mental state overwhelms my vision of the past. My present emotion is like a prism, which alters the shape and colors of my past life."[24] If every presentation is mediated by a mode of representation, we might ask, In what sense is the autobiographer revealing the truth about the self?

Rousseau responds to this problem by saying that even though our memory of objective facts is colored by present feelings and motivations, the essence of the past is nevertheless preserved and made accessible by reporting those feelings. For the essence of the past consists not in *facts* about what occurred, but in the feelings one now has about the past. And those feelings can be called up and expressed at any time in a way that is truthful. So Rousseau writes in his *Confessions*: "I have only one faithful guide on which I can count: the succession of feelings that have marked the development of my being. . . . I may omit or transpose facts, or make mistakes in dates; but I *cannot go wrong about what I have felt* or about what my feelings have led me to do; and these are the chief subjects of my story."[25]

Rousseau here seems to be making a distinction between what we might call *subjective truth* – the truth as it is "for me," relative to my present feelings and commitments – and *objective truth* – the truth about the facts of the matter, regardless of how anyone feels about them. The claim Rousseau makes, then, is that the subjective truth – my truth – is prior to and more fundamental than objective truth. "What is of primary importance is not historical veracity but the emotion experienced as the past emerges and is represented in consciousness."[26] With this shift in emphasis from objective truth to subjective truth, Starobinski says: "We have moved from the realm of (historical) truth to that of *authenticity*" (p. 198).

For the more authentic form of self-revelation Rousseau envisions, what the self-portrait presents is not a faithful copy of the subject but a representation of the subject's ongoing search for the truth of the self. The image is authentic because *the self just is this search*. On the conception of the self that we inherit from Rousseau, self-discovery is not a matter of finding an entity that has been there all along. It is a matter of making the self in the course of the search. What comes to light as authentic truth (i.e., subjective truth) is *the activity of self-fashioning or self-making itself*. We just *are* what we make of ourselves in the course of our quest for self-definition. The important thing is the creative act itself, not objective self-assessment or accurate representation.

Once we have the image of self-discovery formulated by Rousseau, the task of self-knowledge and self-realization can be thought of not merely as similar to artistic creation, but as the ultimate form of artistic creation, the form to which all the other arts, as self-expressions, are subordinate. On this view, everyone is an artist, because each person creates his or her own life, and each person has the ability to create it as a work of art. The project of artistically creating the self requires not self-reflection – which splits apart the reflecting self from the self as object of reflection, a splitting apart that detaches us from life and distorts our vision. Rather, it requires an unreflective immersion in one's own life, a full participation that involves the self as a feeling and acting whole. Rousseau conceives the imperative, "Be yourself," not as telling you to shape yourself according to the requirements of an antecedently given essence, but as directing you to accept that your creative activity of self-making is the ultimate source of your own being. To be yourself, on this view, is to own up to the task of self-making in a way that is truthful to your own genuine feelings at each moment (Starobinski, p. 199). In the end, you will have been whatever you have done in *expressing* yourself in the world. And here it is less important *what* you do than *how* you do it.

One consequence of the nineteenth-century backlash against the domination of science and rationalism was a glorification of art and artistic creativity that is unparalleled in Western culture. Actually, even the very idea of *art* is a relatively new innovation in Western thought. The word "art" had existed for centuries, of course, referring to various skills and fields of learning. But the idea of art as embracing the fine arts seems to have appeared for the first time only in the latter half of the eighteenth century. The term "artist" in its distinctively modern sense, according to the *Oxford English Dictionary*, is even newer. The word *artist*, used to refer to those who held the degree of Master of Arts or to practitioners of such arts as the black arts, had been around for centuries. But the modern use of the word "artist" to refer to those engaged in the arts as we understand them first appears in English only in 1823 with the adoption of the French term, *artiste*. The very idea that there is something that painters and musicians and architects and poets and chefs have in common – something called *being an artist* – is relatively new in Western experience. It seems, then, that the modern idea of art and the concern with becoming authentic grew up around the same time and are very intimately connected.

A beautiful and deeply moving account of what it takes to be an authentic artist is found in Rainer Maria Rilke's *Letters to a Young Poet*. Categorized as a neo-Romantic poet, Rilke is famous for his dark and baffling poetry. But these letters, written to a young, aspiring poet between 1903 and 1908, are exceptionally vivid, and they continue to speak to struggling creative people to this day. The young recipient of the letters, a Franz Xaver Kappus, had sent samples of his poetry to Rilke and expressed his fears about entering a profession, military service, that is so at odds with his goal of being a poet. In his reply, Rilke expresses the deep distrust of social professions and customs that arose with the modern conception of society as something artificial and man-made:

> . . . I can only advise you to consider whether all professions are not like that [Rilke writes], full of demands, full of enmity against the individual, saturated as it were with hatred of those who have found themselves mute and sullen in a humdrum duty. The situation in which you now have to live is no more heavily laden with conventions, prejudices and mistakes than all the other situations, and if there are some that feign a greater freedom, still there is none that is in itself

broad and spacious and in contact with the big things of which real living consists.[27]

To counteract society's pull toward inauthenticity, Rilke proposes a way of life that achieves solitude even in the midst of the world.

Only the individual who is solitary is like a thing placed under profound laws, and when he goes out into the morning that is just beginning, or looks out into the evening that is full of happening, and if he feels what is going on there, then all status drops from him as from a dead man, though he stands in the midst of sheer life. (p. 47)

The authentic self is the individual who can stand alone, shedding all status relations and social entanglements, in order to immerse him- or herself in "sheer life."

The opposition between social existence and actual life provides the framework for the response envisioned in the ideal of becoming authentic. What is required is the ability to disengage oneself from society and its pointless rituals and game-playing, to recoil from all that hypocrisy and pretence, and to turn inward into the innermost self. Rilke describes the way one can, by turning inward, make contact with life, the wider source of being that lies beneath and is distinct from society. The German word for life, Leben, reverberates with evocations of a mystical and supernatural connectedness of all that is. In the picture of authentic existence Rilke paints, we turn inward not for its own sake, but in order thereby to make contact with the deep and primal source of all that is: Life, or Nature, or Being. Far from being something alien to us, life for Rilke is our natural home:

We are set down in life as in the element to which we correspond, and over and above this we have through

> thousands of years of accommodation become so like this life,
> that when we hold still we are, through a happy mimicry,
> scarcely to be distinguished from all that surrounds us.
> We have no reason to mistrust our world, for it is not against
> us. (p. 69)

There is a vision here of the natural order not just as an aggregate of physical objects in causal interactions, but as a living whole in which we, like everything else, have evolved to have a proper place. When we are part of the great flow of life, we are who we truly are. In contrast, when we let ourselves fall prey to social involvements and conventions, we are falling away from our proper place; we are uprooted, groundless and homeless.

How are we to recover our true nature in the scheme of things? We must first strip off all the illusory trappings of social life until we become the solitary individuals we truly are at the core of our being. When we do this, we will become like unto a newborn child.

> To be solitary the way one was solitary as a child, when the
> grownups went around involved with things that seemed
> important and big because they themselves looked so
> busy and because one comprehended nothing of their
> doings.
>
> And when one day one perceives that their occupations are
> paltry, their professions petrified and no longer linked with
> living, why not then continue to look like a child upon it all as
> upon something unfamiliar, from out of the depth of one's
> own world, out of the expanse of one's own solitude, which is
> itself work and status and vocation? Why want to exchange a
> child's wise incomprehension for defensiveness and disdain,
> since incomprehension is after all being alone, while

> defensiveness and disdain are a sharing in that from which
> one wants by these means to keep apart. (p. 46)

Rilke's image of self-fulfillment evokes biblical ideals of becoming childlike, being reborn, and "making foolish the wisdom of the world." But Rilke's vision of authentic existence harks back not to the Judeo-Christian tradition but to more primal, archaic pagan experiences. Life is something we carry within us, and it is up to each of us to cultivate it and express it in our own personal ways.

> Think, dear sir, of the world you carry within you, and call this
> thinking what you will . . . only be attentive to that which rises
> up in you and set it above everything that you observe about
> you. What goes on in your innermost being is worthy of your
> whole love; you must somehow keep working at it and not
> lose too much time and too much courage in clarifying your
> attitude toward people. (p. 47)

What rises up within you – the feelings, responses, thoughts, and desires – is more fundamental – more *real!* – than the objective realities and intersubjective involvements that make up either everyday life or Western traditions. Like Rousseau before him, Rilke envisages a form of subjective truth that is prior to and more genuine than objective truth.

To be an artist, one must become authentic. The artist learns to let the unconscious creative process work itself out in its own way within him, without imposing the assumptions derived from social expectations and reinforced by the intellect. But the converse is also true: to be authentic is to become an artist. For only the creative person can achieve the sort of access to the inner life that captures its depth and potentiality. "*Everything* is gestation and then bringing forth,"

Rilke says. "To let each impression and each germ of a feeling come to completion wholly in itself, in the dark, in the inexpressible, the unconscious, beyond the reach of one's own intelligence, and await with deep humility and patience the birth-hour of a new clarity: that alone is living the artist's life: in understanding and creating" (pp. 29–30).

Becoming an authentic artist requires self-discipline and hard work. One must excise all the opinions of society in order to get in touch with the natural, inner rhythms and pattern of life within oneself. Whereas outer, public time is clock time, the regular ticking away of "nows" as they stretch out endlessly into the future, inner time is the cyclical, organic time of pre-Christian, premodern experience. "There is here no measuring with time, no year matters, and ten years are nothing. Being an artist means, not reckoning and counting, but ripening like the tree which does not force its sap and stands confident in the storms of spring without the fear that after them may come no summer" (p. 30). A sharp opposition is set up here between outer, social life, with its calculating reason and attempts at intellectual mastery, and the inner, authentic life, a life that is organic, mysterious, dark and bound up with some greater reality. The task of the artist is to access the resources hidden deep within the innermost self and to raise them to expression. Artistic creation provides spiritual sustenance and a renewal to a world that has become heartless and cold.

The nineteenth century paid tribute to this conception of art through "the cult of the genius." Where earlier conceptions of the works we now call "artistic" saw the value of such works as lying in their ability to imitate reality or to entertain an audience, the new expressive conception of art drops both the interest in copying reality and the concern with pleasing an audience. All that really matters in art is that the creative genius authentically expresses him- or herself. It is expected that the audience will try to have the right experience in the presence of the work, and with luck a privileged few in the audience may have some inkling of what the genius imparts. But the artist is under no compulsion to communicate anything to anyone – indeed, the concern with communicating now begins to look like a sign that the work is not authentic. Great art is always a slap in the face to the bourgeoisie, because it puts in question the reality of what the bourgeoisie takes as real.

But isn't this the nature of authenticity as such? Isn't it the case that being authentic means being fundamentally and unavoidably out of step with the mainstream? It is hard to see how these questions can be answered in any other way than the affirmative. To be authentic is to be in touch with something that is concealed to the people who accept the outlook of society. At some level, to be authentic is already to be asocial. What is more, being authentic involves having a personal "take" on reality that is "Other" to the social, a deeper reality that is masked by social customs. Insofar as the authentic individual is a creative genius, she will always put her own stamp and interpretation on things. In fact, having a different perspective on things seems to be a criterion of authenticity, for how can one be authentic if one is totally aligned with the herd?

What appears more and more through the nineteenth century, then, is a conception of authentic existence as not merely out of synch with society, but as necessarily antisocial, as something outrageous, perhaps even monstrous. This dark side of authenticity is something Trilling alludes to when he speaks of the "marvelous generative force" attributed to the ideal of authenticity, a force that implies a "downward movement through all the cultural super-structures to some place where all movement ends, and begins." But what if it turns out, as Trilling suggests, that this point of all beginning and ending, this alpha and omega, is "the heart of darkness?"[28]

Five

The rise of the modern worldview set up an opposition between two deeply opposed conceptions of what life is all about. The huge success of the scientific revolution, together with the technological advances that accompanied it, led many to assume that a life guided by procedural reason and a hard-headed attitude concerning reality would guarantee as happy and successful a life as is possible in an uncertain world. These people embraced a conception of life that might be summed up in the slogan, "Better living through rationality." By the beginning of the twentieth century, a slew of books extolling the benefits of living rationally appeared in what we today would call the "self-help" market. One of the best, a little book that is still available and is as compelling now as it was then, is *The Conquest of Happiness* by the philosopher Bertrand Russell. In his cool, sensible, slightly bemused way, Russell suggests that unhappiness is "very largely due to mistaken views of the world."[1] The worst of these mistaken views is the idea that how you are doing is extremely important and a matter for deep concern. To alleviate unhappiness, Russell proposes, you should simply stop thinking about yourself and get active in some worthwhile "objective business" in the world. If you just get busy and do something, you will find that the rest will fall into place by itself.

The opposing conception of life sees the rationalist and instrumentalist view propagated by Russell and others to be arid, heartless, mechanical, and, above all, destructive of the meaningfulness in life. From the standpoint of this more romantically inclined outlook, a life devoted to nothing but *busy-ness* in the social world – to moving unreflectively along the ruts laid out by established practices – is a life that is uprooted from the deeper existential issues at the core of real living. Though functioning in the modern world requires that we be able to perform standardized routines and enact roles, we need something more in life to be really alive at all. What matters most, on this view, is getting in touch with who you really are, developing your talents, blossoming as a creative individual, forming intimate and emotionally fulfilling relationships, and along the way discovering a spiritual dimension to existence.

Though there are people who become obsessed with one or the other of these two paths, most of us strive to realize both dimensions in our lives. In working and in taking care of everyday affairs, we understand both the necessity and advantages of effectively performing routinized tasks and attending to chores in an orderly way. And most of us also see to it that there are enclaves in our lives where we can be, if not artists, at least creative people expressing ourselves in such activities as home decorating, gardening, cooking, shopping, and so on. We handle our day-to-day business in a professional, orderly way, but at the end of the day we look forward to returning to the affectionate embrace of loved ones and to engaging in our own favorite creative activities. Most of us deal with the conflicting demands made on us in the modern world by being instrumentalists in public and Romantics in private.[2] That such an existence is polarized, that it breeds confusions when the private comes to be colonized by instrumentalist tendencies – these are seen as inevitable problems of living under modern circumstances.

What is of interest for our purposes, however, is not so much the compromises we actually make in dealing with the opposition built into modernity as the way this opposition lays out a set of distinctions that structure how we think about our lives. It has often been noted that our ways of thinking and experiencing are shaped by overlapping sets of conceptual distinctions or "binary oppositions" that give us a sense of how things are organized in the world. Without being aware of it, we employ sets of contrasting terms in which each term is defined by its contrast with the opposing term, for example, up/down, front/back, left/right, tall/short, fat/thin, and light/dark. These oppositions articulate and organize the conceptual field in such a way that our perceptions and interpretations tend to follow certain clearly demarcated paths. Because we encounter things through the grid opened up by these binary oppositions, we all tend to operate with a shared, fairly cohesive sense of reality.

What I want to note here is that our modern outlook is shaped by a distinctive set of binary oppositions that governs the way we sort things out in everyday life. As an example of a common binary opposition, consider the way we <u>distinguish artificial and natural.</u> We are all inclined to regard the forms of behavior required in business and professional affairs as in some sense "artificial," while we see the loving attention we give to our children and parents as "natural." Given this opposition, we tend to make a distinction between the *masks* or *personae* we wear in the social arena and the *Real Me* lying beneath the surface of everyday life. The distinction between outward show and inner reality is linked to a distinction we commonly make between our *public* and *private* lives. I tend to suppose that, although in public I have to put on an act, in private I can be myself. As should be apparent, this private/public distinction is correlated with the natural/artificial opposition. The binary oppositions governing our thought lead us to see the natural side of life as pure, spontaneous, and innocent, whereas the social or public side of life is seen as calculating, contrived, tainted, and so deformed and fallen.

These conceptual oppositions in turn map onto the distinctions we make between deep vs. superficial, spiritual vs. materialistic, organic vs. mechanical, genuine vs. fake, true vs. illusory, and original vs. simulation. Sets of binary oppositions lead us to see various contrasts as tied in to others. It is also the nature of binary oppositions that they are 'valorized' in the sense that the terms making up the oppositions are perceived as ranked in such a way that one term of the pair is regarded positively, as referring to something regarded as good or proper, while the other term is regarded negatively, as referring to something derivative or even decadent and degenerate. So, for example, feminists have noted that in a patriarchal society, the masculine is generally treated as what is proper, essential, and genuinely human, whereas the feminine is regarded as derivative, secondary, and "other." (That is why Freud could think that what characterizes women is a "penis envy," the experience of lacking what it takes to be fully human.)

It could be argued that in the modern period the master dichotomy governing all others is the opposition between inner and outer. It seems natural to us to suppose that, with respect to the self, what is inner is what is true, genuine, pure, and original, whereas what is outer is a mere shadow, something derived, adulterated and peripheral. In terms of this conceptual scaffolding, the concept of authenticity is defined by privileging the inner over the outer. To be authentic, you must be in touch with what lies within, that is, the inner self, the self no one sees except you. The inner/outer opposition is clearly valorized: the inner is regarded as higher or more real than the outer. Our outer avowals can be called "authentic" only to the extent that they honestly and fully "express" the inner.

In the modern experience of the self, the ideal trajectory of a life course seems to mirror the ideal life project described by St. Augustine. The movement ought to be "inward and upward." As we understand the notion of authenticity, it is necessary to pull ourselves back from the "outer" realm of worldly preoccupations and encrusted conventions in order to gain access to the "inner" realm of our own private, natural, unspoiled feelings, desires, and goals. Behind this vision of the ideal life trajectory is the assumption that deep within the innermost sanctum of the true self there are resources of insight and truth that are inaccessible to the outer self. What is found within, according to our contemporary view, is a correlate of what premodern people experienced as an enchanted garden: a realm of being filled with meaning because it manifests a power comparable to that of the *mana* or *dharma* of premodern experience. But where earlier people had experienced this purposive and volitional life-force as *out there*, in the Order of Being itself, contemporary experience regards the enchanted garden as *in here, in me*. Deep within me is the True Self, we are inclined to think, a source of mystery, intelligence, and inscrutable will that is concealed from everydayness. For our modern way of thinking, then, one does not turn inward in order to reach something greater than or outside oneself. On the contrary, one turns inward because it is within the innermost self that one discovers the ordinarily unseen and untapped resources of meaning and purpose. For the modern worldview, there is no exit from the circuitry of self; there are only different levels of self.

What is it that lies within? What is this inner self that promises to provide access to the spiritual significance hidden from everyday existence? Ever since the time of Rousseau, the inner/outer dichotomy has been interpreted in terms of the distinction between the child and the adult. What is characteristic of the inner self is that it is childlike, spontaneous, in touch with its own true feelings, and capable of an intuitive understanding of what things are all about. In contrast to the child, the adult self is perceived as hardened and artificial. The adult's feelings are muffled and deformed by playing socially approved games; his or her perceptions are forced into the grids of standardized interpretations. To the modern ear, the New Testament injunction, "Become ye like unto a newborn child," tells us not to purge all traits in order to become a blank slate, but to retrieve and nurture those most childlike and primitive impulses and traits we had in our earliest youth.

When you think of it, this glorification of childhood is quite remarkable. Social historians have shown that the very idea of childhood is a fairly new invention in European civilization. According to Philippe Ariès, medieval Europe seems to have had no clearly defined notion of childhood as a separate period of life. This is evident from the pictorial images of young people in medieval artworks. What we would regard as children or babies were portrayed as short adults. Of course, there were words we can translate as "youth" or "child," but those words were used to refer to social status rather than to an age-group. That is to say, the words were used as women sometimes call a group of friends "the girls," or as a friend in some circles is called "lad" or "child," or as "boy" was used until recently to refer to a servant. Though there were words that seem to refer to an age-group, there was little recognition of childhood as a distinct stage in life, no doubt because in medieval Europe so few children survived the first years of life. Ariès claims that it was not until the sixteenth and seventeenth centuries that there was a "discovery of childhood." The very novelty of the idea justifies the social scientist Anthony Giddens using the expression, the "invention of childhood."[3]

Whatever the origin of the idea of childhood may be, it is now commonly assumed that the child represents human nature in its purest, most essential form. The condition of childhood is the primal source from which all else arises and unfolds. It is the pristine point of origin, the wellspring, the archē. This glorified conception of childhood is coupled with the belief that we are most ourselves when we are in touch with the pre-reflective, spontaneous feelings and responses we experience prior to our indoctrination into adult society. We have already seen how this idea appears in Hölderlin's *Hyperion* and in Rilke's *Letters to a Young Poet*. It is also powerfully expressed in a well-known story, 'The Death of Ivan Ilych,' published in 1886 by the Russian writer Leo Tolstoy. According to this story, Ivan Ilych is a respected magistrate who has been quite successful at doing all the things needed to rise to the top of Russian society. He has a family, a fine home, a successful practice, and a relatively high station in the world. In a way, he looks like Dr. Phil at the time of his moment of vision: he is a success by every external standard. He has it all.

When Ivan Ilych recognizes that he has an incurable illness, he begins to question the value and meaning of his life.

Though Ivan Ilych has always assumed he has lived well and done all the right things, he begins to have a nagging feeling that somehow his life has been wrong, that he has in fact not lived as he ought to have lived. Lying in bed in pain late at night, wishing he could go on enjoying the pleasant life he has had, he hears an "inner voice" asking what sort of life he wants. The answer seems obvious: "Why, to live as I used to – well and pleasantly." Yet now his comfortable and successful life as a professional no longer looks so attractive: "But strange to say none of those best moments of his pleasant life now seemed at all what they had then seemed." As he begins to perceive the falseness of all he has lived for, Ivan Ilych realizes that it is only the experiences of childhood that were pure and spontaneous. "There, in childhood, there had been something really pleasant with which it would be possible to live if it could return. But the child who had experienced that happiness existed no longer."[4]

Reflecting on his life, Ivan Ilych can see it now as a slow and steady descent into the deception, game-playing and corruption of everyday existence:

> And the further he departed from childhood and the nearer he came to the present, the more worthless were the joys. This began with the School of Law. A little that was really good was still found there – there was light-heartedness, friendship, and hope. But in the upper classes there had been fewer of such good moments. Then during the first years of his official career, . . . some pleasant moments again occurred; they were the memories of love for a woman. Then all became confused and there was still less of what was good; later on again there was still less that was good, and the further he went the less there was. (pp. 147–8)

Ivan Ilych now is able to see his whole life as a long day's journey into night: "It is as if I had been going downhill while I imagined I was going up. And that is really what it was. I was going up in public opinion, but to the same extent life was ebbing away from me. And now it is all done and there is only death" (p. 148).

The indictment of social existence is now familiar to us. It is the nature of grown-up life that we are forced to put on masks and play out little games in order to measure up to the demands of the world. But in gaining the world, we lose our souls. We become empty shells, drifting into the monotony and grayness of the commonplace, going through the motions, getting dispersed in the busy-ness of life. In short, we are falling. But there is a prospect for salvation. As a religious writer, Tolstoy describes a moment of redemption that comes at the very last instant of Ivan Ilych's life. When Ivan Ilych finally acknowledges his guilt for having wasted his life, when he makes amends to his family and opens himself to God, he is suddenly opened to a saving light: "In place of death there was light" (p. 156). The message is clear: life is a precious gift, as we instinctively know in childhood; we have an obligation to bring our soul back to its Creator in a state that is pure and undefiled by worldly affairs; we should wear the world as a loose cloak and hold firmly to the spiritual life, no matter what sorts of concessions we are forced to make in order to get by in society. All the ingredients of the religious interpretation of life's aim are in place in Tolstoy: we turn inward in order to get in touch with God; the trajectory is inward and upward; it is by finding God that we are saved.

The religious story told by Tolstoy has become hard to swallow for many people in today's increasingly secularized world.

But the idea that there is a primal truth accessible to the child continues to appear in the work of even the most secular writers. This has been especially true in the area of psychotherapy theory and depth psychology. Indeed, as Anthony Giddens notes, there is a close connection between the emergence of psychotherapy as a cultural institution and the increasing focus on childhood learning and child development in the human sciences. In this new constellation of ideas, "Childhood as a separate sphere becomes an 'infrastructure' of the personality."[5] We find our true nature writ small but clear in our childhood lives.

An especially evocative account of the child as the "true self" can be found in *The Drama of the Gifted Child: The Search for the True Self* by the Swiss psychoanalyst, Alice Miller. Miller begins her book by saying that many of the people who come to her for help are widely admired and respected for what they do. These people "do well, even excellently, in everything they undertake; they are admired and even envied; they are successful whenever they care to be." One would naturally assume that these people have "a strong and stable sense of self-assurance." Nevertheless, as Miller notes, "behind all this lurks depression, a feeling of emptiness and self-alienation, and a sense that life has no meaning. These dark feelings will come to the fore as soon as the drug of grandiosity fails, as soon as they are not 'on top.' . . . Then they are plagued by anxiety or deep feelings of guilt and shame."[6]

What is the cause of this paradoxical condition? In the bland language of psychoanalytic theory, the problem results from a "deficit in parenting." In their childhood, they have failed to receive the sort of parental support they needed and deserved. According to Miller, "every child has a legitimate need to be noticed, understood, taken seriously, and respected by his mother." The reason why this is so important is that the child first comes to discover his own self through the mirroring relation to the primary caregiver. Under optimal conditions, the child gazes into the mother's eyes, the mother gazes back with love and acceptance, and the child then finds himself as mirrored in her gaze (p. 27).

Things go wrong, according to this story, when the mother is unable to accept the child as he or she really is at any given time. "When we speak here of 'the person she really is at any given time,' " Miller says, "we mean emotions, sensations, and their expression from the first day onward" (p. 6). When such acceptance is not available, the individual suffers an "inability to experience consciously certain feelings as his own (such as jealousy, envy, anger, loneliness, or anxiety), either in childhood or later in adulthood" (p. 9). When the child's expressions of feelings meet disapproval on the part of the parent, the child learns to stop experiencing those feelings. The "true self," the self that experiences a range of natural feelings, tends to be covered up. In its place, the child learns to manifest a self that expresses and experiences the feelings which meet approval. As a result, a "false self" dominates the personality. As an example of a false self we might imagine, depending on the desires and expectations of the parent, a smiley, "people pleaser" self or a serious, sensible, unemotional self.

When there is a deficit in parenting, the child's formation of a self occurs as an accommodation to parental needs. The result is an "as-if personality."

This person develops in such a way that he reveals only what is expected of him and fuses so completely with what he reveals that one could scarcely guess how much more there is to him behind this false self. He cannot develop and differentiate his true self, because he is unable to live it. Understandably, this person will complain of a sense of emptiness, futility, or homelessness, for the emptiness is real. A process of emptying, impoverishment, and crippling of his potential actually took place. The integrity of the child was injured when all that was alive and spontaneous in him was cut off. (pp. 11–12)

As such an individual grows up, "he is still dependent on affirmation from his partner, from groups, and especially from his own children" (p. 13).

What is the solution for the problem of growing up into a false self? In a section of her book called "In Search of the True Self," Miller says that the person who has never received the affirmation and support he so richly deserved will simply have to accept this fact. Trying to receive the sort of support a parent owes to a child from an adult partner is doomed to failure – no adult can or should provide such support to another adult. In the end, Miller sees maturity and healing as coming with the ability to mourn: "The paradise of pream-bivalent harmony, for which so many patients hope, is unattainable. But the experience of one's own truth . . . make[s] it possible to return to one's own world of feelings at an adult level – without paradise, but with the ability to mourn" (p. 14).

One can recognize that one has been cheated out of one's childhood. "What became of my childhood?" one asks. "I can never return to it. I can never make up for it. From the begin-ning I have been a little adult" (p. 14). With this recognition of irrevocable loss, followed by a suitable period of grieving, the individual can achieve a maturity that makes it possible to realize the true self that has been concealed all these years. The patient reaches "a new empathy with her own fate, born out of mourning," and realizes that she can feel and express emotions such as anger and envy without shame: "I can be sad or happy whenever anything makes me sad or happy; I don't have to look cheerful for someone else. . . . I can be angry and no one will die or get a headache because of it. I can rage when you hurt me, without losing you" (p. 15). The mature individual now is capable of "the freedom to experience spontaneous feelings." "It is part of the kaleidoscope of life," Miller says, "that these feelings are not only happy, beautiful, or good but can reflect the entire range of human experience, including envy, jealousy, rage, disgust, greed, despair, and grief" (pp. 60–1). Maturity means accepting the bad with the good.

"Without paradise," but with the ability to press onward in a grown-up way, recognizing and expressing one's ownmost feelings, with neither fear of disapproval nor a desire to please. One sheds the masks and game-playing of the inauthentic "false self" and achieves the "healthy self-feeling" that comes from "the unquestioning certainty that the feelings and needs one experiences are part of one's own self" (p. 28). It would be hard to imagine either a more straightforward account of authentic existence or a more promising vision of life for people suffering from lack of self-esteem or from lack of a clear sense of identity.

Miller's vision of life embodies a number of familiar assumptions about the human condition. First, there is the assumption that the elemental feelings and needs of early childhood define our true identity as humans. We enter the world as bundles of feelings that make up the true self. From the outset, we need to have those feelings validated. If they are

so inherent
the true self can be damaged?

not validated, we will develop a warped and distorted false self. Second, there is the assumption that feelings are inherently okay, that there are no intrinsically bad feelings. This is a view found frequently in the writings of psychotherapy theorists – consider, for example, this comment from therapist Janet Woititz: "Feelings are not RIGHT or WRONG. They just are. . . . Maybe there are certain ways we should not behave, but feelings have no right or wrong value."[7] Hatred, vengefulness, spite, resentment and murderous rage are not bad, though "maybe" acting on such feelings could be bad. Third, there is a valorization of the infant's experience over the adult's. Miller clearly assumes that there is something right and good about having and expressing the kinds of feelings and spontaneous responses characteristic of the young child. Finally, Miller seems to assume that living the fullest and healthiest life requires the ability to experience and express the feelings that naturally arise within us. To be like unto a newborn child is to be able to feel and act in a childlike way without feeling guilt or shame. Throughout her reflections, Miller relies on a set of valorized binary oppositions that contrast childhood, understood as what is natural, inner and positive, with what is grown-up, external, artificial and negative.

The first thing to note in considering Miller's picture is that we have come a long way from traditional understandings of life. Certainly this is a long way off from Aristotle, who insists that what is important is not to have feelings and act on them, but to cultivate and discipline oneself so that one has the right feelings in the right situations at the right time.[8] What we find in older ways of thinking is not the belief that the authentic traits of humanity are those that characterize childhood. Instead, there is the assumption that to be human is to be

under way in an ongoing course of development and formation in which the childish and infantile comes to be cultivated
through education and self-discipline in order to realize the
goal of being a mature, fully formed, responsible citizen in
a *polis*.

A second thing to note is the way Miller unquestioningly
assumes that the self is to be understood as a mind or sphere
of consciousness, where this is thought of as a sort of receptacle
containing experiences such as feelings, desires and needs. In
the full flowering of the modern worldview, the self is
regarded as what we earlier called a "subject of inwardness,"
a center of experience and will that has no necessary or
ineradicable relations to anything outside itself. Given such a
view of the self, the issue of living the best possible life is
regarded as a matter of trying to consolidate and strengthen
that inner self to ensure an accord between the experiences
within the subjective sphere and the outer manifestations of
those experiences in the public world. In the vocabulary used
by Philip Cushman, the goal of self-realization involves
becoming a "bounded, masterful, self-encapsulated self,"[9] a
self that is empowered, free from illusions and able to function without prolonged experiences of dysphoria (i.e., feeling
bad about things). There is no room in such a picture for any
notion of being obligated to behave in a civil way in public, to
have the decency to contain your feelings out of consideration for others, or to concentrate on what you contribute to a
situation rather than on how the situation affects your feelings. One might begin to suspect that the true self envisioned
by Miller runs the risk of being maddeningly self-absorbed
and selfish, constantly obsessed with herself, unable to let go
and simply be part of the flow of things.

Miller's vision of the true self makes manifest one of the

pervasive features of contemporary thinking about life: the tendency to *psychologize* the issues of living, to see them in the light of the powerful discipline of psychology that has grown up over the past hundred years or so. This psychologized interpretation of life has trickled down into the speech and responses of everyday life. In an essay titled "Civility and Psychology," Harvard child psychiatrist Robert Coles describes the way that discourse in America is now overrun with talk about "what works for me," "where I'm coming from," and "what makes him tick." "The hallmark of our time," Coles writes, "seems to be lots of psychological chatter, lots of self-consciousness, lots of 'interpretations.' As the saying goes, 'Let it all hang out,' and then we'll 'talk about it.' "[10] Here "psychology" refers not to the professional discipline, but to a pervasive concern with the inner self: "Psychology, in this instance, means a concentration, persistent, if not feverish, upon one's thoughts, feelings, wishes, worries – bordering on, if not embracing, solipsism: the self as the only or main form of (existential) reality" (p. 189). What is left in the dust by this psychologization of the issues of living is an older concern with *civility* in one's dealings with others. Civility, with its "sense that one's behavior ought to be, under a range of circumstances, responsive to, respectful of, certain standards" (p. 191), now looks like inauthenticity.

Alice Miller is confident that getting in touch with and expressing one's inner feelings and needs – the feelings and needs of the child, including those that still lie below the surface in adults – will ensure a better life for the individual. With her optimistic appraisal of authentic existence, she represents a strand of psychology that sees what is given in the inner self as having only positive contributions to make to

Miller
ideology

one's existence. In contrast, a different strand of psychological theory has been much more suspicious of the primal forces lying beneath the surface of everyday social existence. These alternative readings of the inner life de-stabilize the binary oppositions that frame our ordinary ways of thinking about authenticity.

A particularly interesting example of an alternative conception of the inner is the thought of the Swiss depth psychologist, Carl G. Jung. Though there are many dimensions to Jung's thought, it will be worthwhile for our purposes to focus on a side of Jung recently brought to light by Richard Noll in his biographical work, *The Aryan Christ: The Secret Life of Carl Jung.* According to Noll, Jung was always distrustful of the rationalized and calculating outlook of modern science and was fascinated by the archaic experience of life found in ancient mystery cults and myths. It would be a mistake, Jung thought, to try to make the helping professions into sciences, because science itself is the source of many of the pathologies of modern humanity. Science "is part of the disease, not the cure."[11] What is needed to heal the damage done by rationalism and scientism, in Jung's view, is not more science, but instead a new religion that will take the place of the now defunct Judeo-Christian worldview.

Asked by Freud in 1910 whether psychoanalysis should associate itself with an ethical fraternity, Jung replied that "2000 years of Christianity can only be replaced by something equivalent, an 'irresistible mass movement.' "[12]

> I imagine a far finer and more comprehensive task for
> [psychoanalysis] than alliance with an ethical fraternity. I
> think we must give it time to infiltrate into people from many
> centers, to revivify among intellectuals a feeling for symbol

and myth, ever so gently to transform Christ back into the soothsaying god of the vine, which he was, and in this way absorb those ecstatic instinctual forces of Christianity for the *one* purpose of making the cult and the sacred myth what they once were – a drunken feast of joy where man regained the ethos and holiness of an animal. That was the purpose and beauty of classical religion.[13]

In the earliest times, Jung suggests, Christ was originally the "god of the vine," Dionysus, and the religious life was "a drunken feast of joy" aimed at bringing people back to the pattern of life (*ethos*) of the prehuman animal. This older experience of the religious life has been lost as Christianity has grown into the repressive, stultifying religion it now is.

Psychoanalysis should aim at peeling off the hardened layers of moralism and intellectualism that have grown over life in order to recover the primal sources from which real living springs. The Jungian version of depth psychology is grounded in a sharp distinction between the archaic inner self, what millennia of Judeo-Christian repression have pushed into the unconscious, and the trappings of scientific, rational and "ethical" society as they are found in the public world of ordinary practical affairs. The outer, conscious level of life is suffocating, deadening to the spirit; it is nihilistic in that it constricts the spontaneous drives and visions that make up our natural inheritance as a species. Psychoanalysis shows people how to turn away from the mechanical and contrived outlook of contemporary life and turn inward to rediscover the "gods" (or, later, "archetypes") they carry within them. The path to redemption (what Jung later called "individuation") requires a descent into the unconscious mind that will reintroduce the individual to the forgotten sources of being.

"For those who survived an encounter with the god or gods within, Jung promised rebirth as a true 'individual,' free from all the repressive mechanisms of conventional beliefs about family, society, and deity. The successful survivors of such pagan regeneration became reborn, spiritually superior 'individuated' beings."[14]

It should be evident that Jung expands and transforms the binary oppositions that shape our contemporary thinking about life. Onto the familiar distinctions of natural/artificial and childlike/disillusioned, he grafts a set of distinctions that include pagan/Christian, Dionysian/rationalistic, instinctual/scientific, creative/calcified, and, above all, unconscious/conscious. What is intensified in Jung's interpretation of these dichotomies is the distrust – even contempt – for civilization and its achievements. In his view, civilization has ruined people, forcing them into cramped, artificial urban environments and suffocating their creative powers with hyperconscious reflection. Civilization, rationality and science are described in a vocabulary that employs metaphors of degeneration and decay. Seeing nearly all of modern civilization as decadent, Jung sets out to recover the mystical union of a people with its blood and soil. As Noll puts it, "The iron cage of 'civilization' – Judeo-Christian beliefs and other political and value systems – had to be cast off in order to recover true culture, the primordial ground of the soul, the *Volk* [people]. There was only one solution: recover the 'archaic man' within, allowing a rejuvenating return to the chthonic powers of the Edenic, Aryan past" (p. 115).

Jung continues to give a positive valorization to the inner and childlike. Within the reaches of the unconscious, each of us carries insights into the original and true nature of life. But these insights have been covered over with the distortions and obfuscation created by civilization, the understanding of things that dominates our conscious minds. To get in touch with the inner self, then, is to gain access to the wisdom, mysteries and sense of purpose built into a "collective unconscious." By retrieving this archaic wisdom, we can be transformed into higher, more "individuated" beings. In this process, we will also come to be (in the words of one of Jung's heroes, Nietzsche) "beyond good and evil." For the transformed individual, the moral ideals and teachings of the Western tradition will no longer have any binding authority. In fact, they now are seen to be repressive, arbitrary impositions that block us from being all we can be. The ideal for Jung, then, is to cast off this entire social and ethical tradition in order to realize and express the inner truth that has been concealed. What lies within us provides the resources for rejuvenation and regeneration. But it also seems to be the source of amoral and frightening capacities and drives. The inner turns out to be, by all the criteria of "civilized" morality, something dangerous, untamed and potentially destructive.

Where Jung's vision of the inner life makes us feel uncomfortable, the view of Jung's contemporary and early mentor, Sigmund Freud, is deeply unnerving. Unlike Jung, Freud was very much a product of the radical Enlightenment, a firm believer in science and its methods of explanation. Intent on naturalizing human phenomena, he set out to describe what he called the "psychic apparatus" and to provide causal accounts of how it works. According to his mature view of the mind, the self consists of three distinct agencies or personality subsystems, each with its own functions and characteristics. It is crucial to Freud's view that the self we are ordinarily aware of in everyday life – the thinking, planning, perceiving and acting self – is only a small part of who we really are. This conscious self Freud calls the *ego*. The ego serves an executive function: it is the seat of practical reasoning and it engages in cost/benefit analyses as it tries to find means of realizing its ends in the world.

More original and fundamental than the ego is the unconscious part of the self, the subsystem called the *id*. The id is present from birth and contains the basic drives Freud calls the "primary processes," the drives to eat, drink and defecate, as well as the natural drive to bisexuality within everyone. Its workings generally remain unconscious, though they may become manifest in feelings such as anxiety, ambivalence, pleasure and pain. The id (in German, the *Es* or "it") is the "other" to all conscious thinking and planning. A vast reservoir of energy pushing us to satisfy basic needs and drives, it works "behind our backs" in the sense that we are not aware of what it is making us do. So, in the most obvious example, we are under pressure to preserve the species by having sexual intercourse, but we generally experience this drive not in this crude form, but rather as being "attracted" to someone and finding him or her "nice to be with." All the activities of courting and marriage in the social world, then, are just a cover-up for what is really going on inside us: a raw, mindless, amoral drive to copulate and reproduce.

In Freud's scheme of things, the id is the Real Me – the authentic self that lies beneath the surface of ordinary polite social existence. As Freud says, "we are 'lived' by unknown and uncontrollable forces" that make us do the things we do.[15] In contrast, the ego – the social and conscious self – is merely an appendage that is added on to the id in the course of its development. Freud writes, "We shall now look at an individual as a psychical id, unknown and unconscious, upon

A supposed
distraction

whose surface rests the ego," and he accompanies this claim with a diagram portraying the perceiving and conscious part of the self as a sort of pimple growing on one side of the massive id (EI 17–18). Elsewhere he says that the ego is "a façade" for the id, suggesting that the ego, as the means by which one presents the self in the world, is a sort of false face or mask designed as much to conceal the true self as to let it be manifest.[16]

The functioning of the id is determined by what Freud calls the "pleasure principle." This is Freud's version of the idea, formulated by the utilitarians during the radical Enlightenment, that people always act with the aim of maximizing pleasure and minimizing pain. Freud's version of the pleasure principle takes as its model the standard reflex arc, that is, the causal circuit between stimulus and response that connects, for example, itching to scratching or nasal membrane irritation to sneezing. The result is a very simple picture of human motivation. On this account, when excitation of some sort is introduced into the psychic apparatus, pressure is created to release the excitation through motor activity. So, returning to the classic example, when we feel sexual desire, we feel an urge to release it through sexual activity. In Freud's scheme of things, pain is nothing other than pent-up excitation in the psychic system, and pleasure is nothing other than a release of that excitation leading to a return to homeostatic equilibrium.

This picture of what motivates us to act has a peculiar corollary. From the claim that there is a constant pressure in the psychic apparatus to release all energy and return to equilibrium, Freud proposes that there must be a deep-seated drive in all living things to reach complete and final quiescence. Since the total release of all energy is achieved only in death, there must be a powerful instinct in all organisms to reach death. These reflections, together with attempts to explain such phenomena as masochism and ambivalence, led Freud to posit the existence of a *death instinct* in all living things. In his mature psychological theory, Freud sees human action as arising from a dynamic interplay of two conflicting sets of instincts: the sexual and life-preserving drives (*Eros*) and the death instinct (*Thanatos*).

Because the death instinct is so fundamentally opposed to the life instinct, it is normally subject to a "reversal of direction" in people. That is to say, it is directed not inward toward the self, but outward toward others so that it becomes an instinct of destructiveness. In Freud's view, the death instinct explains why humans tend to be so aggressive and cruel in their relations with one another and with nature as a whole. The truth is, Freud says,

> men are not gentle creatures who want to be loved, . . . they are, on the contrary creatures among whose instinctual endowments is to be reckoned a powerful share of aggressiveness. As a result, their neighbor is for them not only a potential helper or sexual object, but also someone who tempts them to satisfy their aggressiveness on him, to exploit his capacity for work without compensation, to use him sexually without his consent, to seize his possessions, to humiliate him, to cause him pain, to torture and to kill him. (*CD* 69)

Freud has the courage to take an unblinking look at the capacity for cruelty and destructiveness in humans: Man "is a savage beast to whom consideration towards his own kind is something alien" (CD 69). Though we generally try to cover up these darker drives with the veneer of polite, civil behavior, there is a capacity for cruelty and violence below the surface that is part of our basic human endowment. It is a capacity that is manifest in the sensual, almost voluptuous pleasure people feel when the door is opened to torturing and humiliating others. It is evident in catty remarks and in the *Schadenfreude* we feel when we see others' hopes dashed. And it is even more evident in the horrors of the Holocaust, in the atrocities of dictators such as Hitler, Stalin, Pol Pot, Idi Amin or Saddam Hussein, and in the actions, reported in the newspapers on a daily basis, of "ordinary folks" who starve and beat and shame their children.

Freud claims that the capacity for aggression is something "we can detect in ourselves and justly assume to be present in others" (CD 69). Writing on this topic forty years before Freud's *Civilization and Its Discontents*, Dostoevsky gives an especially poignant description of the capacity for cruelty in all people. One of the characters in *The Brothers Karamazov*, after describing the pleasure a father takes in beating his young daughter with a birch rod, says, "I know for a fact there are people who at every blow are worked up to sensuality, to literal sensuality, which increases progressively at every blow they inflict. They beat for a minute, for five minutes, for ten minutes, more often and more savagely. The child screams. At last the child cannot scream; it gasps, 'Daddy! Daddy!' "[17] And in case we feel that this is just what some demented "others" do, Dostoevsky's character insists that we all have within us such a capacity for finding sensual pleasure in hurting others: "In every man, of course, a demon lies hidden, the demon of rage, the demon of lustful heat at the screams of the tortured victim, the demon of lawlessness let off the chain" (ibid).

Freud sums up his conception of the primordiality of aggression in humans with the ancient formula, *Homo homini lupus*, "Man is a wolf to man." It is because cruelty and aggression are the bedrock of human nature that civilization has to take such extreme measures to control people's natural instincts. It is the function of every civilization to impose laws and regulations aimed at restricting and repressing instinctual behavior. This process is abetted by the formation in humans of a moral sense through the emergence of the *superego*, an internalized sense of a moral authority that promises punishment for infractions of the moral code. The superego is the source of guilt feelings people feel, often to exaggerated and irrational degrees, and it is also the source of the idea of a Higher Power or supreme Father figure who judges us for our sins.

The superego is the "harsh taskmaster" (EI 53) that supports society's project of restraining individuals and keeping them in line. Freud's vision of social existence is in line with the outlook of social contract theorists from Hobbes, Locke and Rousseau to today. What is "given" – the basic fact about human reality – is a collection of self-encapsulated individuals, each with his or her own drives, needs and aims, with no real or essential relations to anything outside themselves. Society (or "civilization") therefore must be understood as an artificial construct invented in order to regulate the behavior of those individuals. With its prohibitions and constraints, its aim is the renunciation of instinct; it prevents the free and open expression of sexual cravings and constrains the hostility that inevitably arises among humans. In the process of restricting and repressing natural desires, however, civilization creates guilt feelings and anxieties that ultimately make civilized humans miserable. Freud fully agrees with the contention, suggested by Rousseau and others, "that what we call our civilization is largely responsible for our misery, and that we should be much happier if we gave it up and returned to primitive conditions" (CD 38). Civilization is the main source of the neuroses that enslave us and make life so painful. Even worse, in providing us with security and stability, civilization also deprives us of freedom: "The liberty of the individual is no gift of civilization," Freud says; freedom "was greatest before there was any civilization" (CD 49).

Freud's response to this sad situation is basically to say "Get used to it." We cannot live without civilization, and we cannot find happiness within civilization. In place of the valorized binary oppositions that frame the ideal of authenticity, we find only the ambivalent and unstable oppositions of Freud's "No win" situation. With his cold, clear eye, Freud looks out over the suffering created by the conflicting demands of life and recommends grim, Stoic resignation. The message is: "survive, resign yourself to living within your moral means, suffer no gratuitous failures in a futile search for ethical heights that no longer exist – if they ever did."[18] Freud's final estimation of our situation expresses the tired wisdom of the healer who knows the disease has no cure. "Thus I have not the courage to rise up before my fellow-men as a prophet," Freud concludes, "and I bow to their reproach that I can offer them no consolation" (CD 111).

Freud's recognition of the heart of darkness that lies within each of us puts a new spin on the idea of authenticity. The bland assurance that all humans are basically good by nature, together with the assumption that it is only society that makes them bad, is no longer tenable. Freud has shown us that deep within us there is a mixed bag of capacities and drives, some of them kind and loving, others dark and cruel. Nor is it necessary to buy into Freud's weird notion of the death instinct to accept the inescapable reality of aggression and violence as essential to the human animal. The same point is made by the Nobel-prize-winning Austrian natural scientist Konrad Lorenz in his book, *On Aggression*, a study of the "killer instinct" in all animals that shows why human beings can feel righteousness even as they commit atrocities.[19] And William Golding's classic novel, *The Lord of the Flies*, gives us a convincing picture of the capacity for cruelty and brutality in children who have been separated from social constraints. Given the accumulated evidence on the centrality of aggressiveness in humanity's natural endowment, Rousseau's naïve faith that human beings are naturally good has lost its plausibility. The enchanted garden, now internalized in the innermost self, is found to be filled with monstrous and terrifying forces.

Recognizing our capacity for evil can undermine our assurance that we will necessarily live a good life if we get in touch with and express our innermost, primal selves. From this standpoint, the distrust of the social circumstances of life in the older conception of authenticity now seems problematic. Society may inhibit and repress us, it seems, but it is also the only thing standing between us and "The Horror" Kurtz saw in Joseph Conrad's *The Heart of Darkness*. Though we have good traits within us, the only way to disentangle those traits from traits we regard as mean and despicable is by using a moral map that clearly marks out right and wrong. And that map is something we get from our socialization. Society, far from being the enemy of goodness, turns out to be its only hope.

Of course, there is another reading of the significance of the heart of darkness within, a reading that has shaped a sort of counter-culture to the dominant culture of authenticity in contemporary society. This counter-culture encourages us to accept the fact that what lies within is characterized by aggression, cruelty and violence, and holds that authenticity is precisely a matter of getting in touch with and expressing those dark impulses and cravings. The idea that being authentic is a matter of venting all that is brutal and ugly in the inner self, originating in the work of such pivotal figures as the Marquis de Sade, Arthur Rimbaud, Georges Bataille and Antonin Artaud, now has come to play a central role in certain lifestyle enclaves of Western culture. It appears in the "Theater of the Absurd" and the "Theater of Cruelty," in the Beat poetry of the fifties – for example, in Allen Ginsberg's "Howl" – and it shows up again and again in Heavy Metal and punk rock, in gangsta' rap and slam poetry, and in styles of art that quite consciously set out to be a "slap in the face" to the bourgeoisie.

Seen from this angle, to be authentic is to openly express all the rage, raw sexuality and cruelty within you, even when (perhaps I should say "especially when") doing so flies in the face of cultivated morality and manners. In his classic work of a half century ago, Lionel Trilling marked out the smooth path leading from skepticism about social life to the outrageous flouting of social norms in the name of madness and violence. Given the idea of authenticity, he writes, "much that was once thought to make up the very fabric of culture has come to seem of little account, mere fantasy and or ritual, or downright falsification. Conversely, much that culture traditionally condemned and sought to exclude is accorded a considerable moral authority by reason of the authenticity claimed for it, for example, disorder, violence, unreason."[20] The glorification of disorder and violence in today's society, especially in the youth culture, receives its justification from the ideal of authenticity just as does the mild-mannered decency promoted by Oprah and Dr. Phil. Both visions of

Media conversions

authentic existence start out from an ideal of "downward movement through all the cultural superstructures to some place where all movement ends, and begins."[21] But the violence and unreason found at the source according to this conception of authenticity is a far cry from what is presupposed by Oprah and Dr. Phil.

Six

It might be helpful to sum up the train of thought developed so far. We are asking whether the concept of authenticity as we currently use it really makes sense. This question has been sharpened by contrasting premodern and modern ways of thinking. We saw that in premodern societies there is a notion similar in some ways to our notion of authenticity – the idea of realizing the purposes laid out by nature or by God – and we saw that this idea makes sense because of the way it fits into the conceptual net that is characteristic of traditional worldviews. By way of contrast, the last three chapters have shown how the traditional conceptual structure has been dismantled in the modern period, and how this de-structuring undermines the ideal of realizing a purpose given us in the scheme of things. We saw, first of all, that the traditional tripartite constellation – "man–nature–God" – is displaced by the modern anthropocentric picture of humans as being independent of both nature and God. And second, we saw how the valorized binary oppositions that initially provided the scaffolding for the modern idea of authenticity have been de-stabilized and upset by the revisionary trends of the past century or so. As a result of these conceptual shifts, it is no longer possible to assume that getting in touch with and expressing what lies within will ensure that you are living a good, fulfilling and meaningful life.

how is it ensured

Another way to describe the transition from premodern to modern is to say that whereas the premodern worldview understood human existence in terms of the image of an extended self, the modern worldview understands humans as nuclear selves. To be human, on this view, is to be a self-contained, bounded individual, a center of experience and will, with no essential or defining relations to anything or anyone outside oneself. Philosophers have labeled the self so regarded a *subject*. To be human, according to the modern way of thinking, is to be a subject, a sphere of subjectivity containing its own experiences, opinions, feelings and desires, where this sphere of inner life is only contingently related to anything outside itself.

Though the subject is conceived of as a simple and unified phenomenon, the concept of the subject as understood by philosophers and social scientists is complex and embraces a number of characteristics:

1   The subject is defined as an "inner space" – it is a mind or field of consciousness containing such mental contents as perceptions, interpretations, memories, feelings, desires, goals and needs. Its relation to the "outer," material world is mediated by those mental contents (e.g., the sensations received through the senses and the actions implemented through goal-setting and choice). Being the arena of thought and experience, it is what one refers to when one uses words such as "I" or "ego."

2   The subject is the source from which action springs. As an agent, the ultimate initiator of action, it is free in the sense that it can determine its own goals and decide its own course of action.

3 A subject is capable of self-reflection and self-consciousness: it monitors its own activity and engages in an ongoing internal monologue (called "thinking") about what it is doing.

4 The subject is self-subsistent, distinct from everything outside itself, including its own body. To be a subject is to be capable of objectifying and working over aspects of one's situation, one's body, even one's own feelings and desires, on the basis of rational reflection about what one wants to attain. *poses a question*

5 The ultimate task set for the subject is to work itself over in order to achieve self-fulfillment or self-realization, however this is conceived.

The self as conceived in modernity is a "bounded, masterful self," what Joseph Dunne calls the "sovereign self."[1] The notion of the subject has been central to theories of knowledge, ethical theories, accounts of social relations developed by political scientists, and psychological theories such as ego psychology and mainstream forms of psychotherapy. Thinking of the self as a subject has been central to modern thought. But the concept of the subject has also come under sustained attack in the last half century from a cluster of movements loosely termed postmodern. One of the core ideas of postmodernism is "de-centering the subject," where this means rethinking humans as polycentric, fluid, contextual subjectivities, selves with limited powers of autonomous choice and multiple centers with diverse perspectives. With its radical undermining of the very notion of a cohesive self, it would seem that this postmodern outlook leaves nothing for the ideal of authenticity to stand on. Yet many thinkers hold that, like the phoenix, the ideal of authenticity rises afresh from the conflagration of postmodernism. This is what we now have to see.

Long before postmodernism came on the scene, psychologists and philosophers were aware that selfhood can be experienced in ways that express multiple standpoints rather than a single point of view. In his book *Composing the Soul*, Graham Parkes notes that as early as 1890 the American psychologist William James, reflecting on the multiplicity of roles people play, considered the possibility that a normal, healthy individual might be seen as containing multiple selves and not just as wearing multiple masks. In *The Principles of Psychology* James writes,

> Properly speaking, *a man has as many social selves as there are [groups of] individuals who recognize him* and carry an image of him in their mind. . . . He generally shows a different side of himself to each of these different groups. . . . We do not show ourselves to our children as to our club-companions, to our customers as to the laborers we employ, to our own masters and employers as to our intimate friends. From this there results what practically is a division of the man into several selves; and this may be a discordant splitting, as where one is afraid to let one set of his acquaintances know him as he is elsewhere; or it may be a perfectly harmonious division of labor, as where one tender to his children is stern to the soldiers or prisoners under his command.[2]

On any given day I am a father to my children, a husband to my wife, a teacher to my students, a customer to various businesses, a colleague to my co-workers, an American Idol contestant in the shower, and a plaything to my cat. Each of these identities involves a distinctive orientation, mindset, temperament, and style.

The commonly accepted interpretation of this phenomenon is that I am adopting different masks appropriate to different contexts. This seems to be the meaning of Shakespeare's words quoted in Chapter 3: "All the world's a stage, / And all the men and women merely players; / They have their exits and their entrances; / And one man in his time plays many parts."[3] Here we find the familiar idea that there is one self playing many parts. In opposition to this older conception of life, James considers the possibility that it is not necessarily *one man* who is playing all the different parts that make up a life. Following James' lead, we might ask whether there is any reason to assume there must be an unequivocal answer to the question: Which of these many parts is the real me? Or, assuming that the real me is none of these roles, we might ask whether there is any reason to think there must be an answer to the question: What is the real me that lies beneath all these roles? We are inclined to think that there must be an "I" behind the masks who is running the show, rather like the little man behind the curtain in *The Wizard of Oz*. But is there really any good reason to assume there must be an "I" who is in charge? The more we reflect on this assumption, the more the belief in the substantial "I" begins to look dubious.

James held that we all need to find a defining role, a central character, if we are going to be fully human. He notes that, for real people, not all things are possible. Stepping back from my life, I might fantasize about being a world traveler or a monk, a married man or a Casanova, a high-powered businessman or a philosopher, a body builder or a bookish intellectual. But given the choices I have made at any time, I have limited the range of options open to me. Having assumed certain concrete possibilities, others are for ever foreclosed. Even given my limited range of possibilities, however, I can ask: Which of these roles is the real me? Am I a teacher who dabbles in music or a musician trying to make ends meet by teaching? James concludes that one simply has to make a leap, embracing one role as the defining one and letting the others fall to the sidelines. "So the seeker of his truest, strongest, deepest self must review the list carefully, and pick out the one on which to stake his salvation. All other selves thereupon become unreal."[4]

But now the question arises: Why must there be a *single self* on which "to stake one's salvation?" Isn't it possible to simply let whatever self is playing its part at the moment occupy center stage and do its own thing? Writing shortly before James, Nietzsche was willing to adopt just such a view. "The assumption of one single subject is perhaps unnecessary," Nietzsche suggests, "perhaps it is just as permissible to assume a multiplicity of subjects, whose interaction and struggle is the basis of our thinking and our consciousness."[5] On this suggestion, the unified point of view we call the "I" might be the by-product of a multiplicity of interacting and competing forces operating "behind our backs" to create the so-called "self" we present in everyday life. Filling out this strand of thought, Nietzsche imagines someone who is content to experience his spirit and his heart as "constantly transforming itself anew, and who . . . is happy to harbor within him not 'an immortal soul' but rather *many mortal souls*."[6] Not one immortal soul, as claimed by the Christian tradition and the metaphysical tradition it spawned, but rather "many mortal souls," many identities inhabiting one body and showing themselves to greater or lesser degrees in the public arena, many characters making their entrances and exits as the context demands.

If it is possible to imagine a human being as an unfolding, centerless play of persons, it is possible to see the "I" – the self-aware, supposedly unified subject said to underlie the ensemble of personalities – as merely one more mask, one more "self" among all the others, with no privileged status or authority. Certainly there are contexts in which the "I" should take center stage and be in charge – when signing a contract, for instance, or when making vows. But the fact that the "I" or ego sometimes has a place in the rich pageantry of life is no reason to think it is the "Real Me" in any sense. James Hillman suggests that the mark of the "I" is usually a cover for an archetypal figure, the figure of the "hero," whose muscular assertion and hands-on approach is appropriate to some situations but not others. There are too many contexts where it is best to keep the ego out of the center of action, where it only creates havoc. As Parkes puts it: in most cases there is no reason to let the ego upstage the other characters or play the role of director.[7]

Although earlier thinkers explored the idea of a variety of selves inhabiting one body, postmodern thinkers concentrate on the way a variety of external forces, unbeknownst to us, work to condition or shape our ways of thinking and acting. An influential strand of this postmodern outlook is social and linguistic constructionism. Constructionism is the view that there is a tacit understanding of reality built into the social practices and language we absorb in becoming initiated into a specific community. This understanding is said to "construct" our ways of encountering things, including our own identities as persons. The influence of society in constructing our self-understanding is evident when we look at the way a child growing up into a particular social context comes to internalize the standardized interpretations deposited in the linguistic categories and norm-governed practices of its community. By the time the child is old enough to function as a participant in the communal life, its understanding of reality, including its sense of what it is to be human, is formed and defined in ways judged "normal" in its social context. The outcome of this process of socialization is an adult who sorts things out and identifies objects in ways that are generally in tune with the public world.

One seminal figure in the rise of social constructionism is the American anthropologist, Clifford Geertz. In his influential essay of 1966, "The Impact of the Concept of Culture on the Concept of Man," Geertz draws together discoveries in anthropology and human physiology to show the central role cultural information plays in the formation of a human being. In opposition to the Enlightenment belief in a common human nature underlying all forms of human culture, Geertz shows that humans are essentially incomplete animals who are dependent on cultural meanings to be able to achieve a determinate, functioning condition. As Geertz says, "man is, in physical terms, an incomplete, an unfinished animal; . . . what sets him off most graphically from nonmen is less his sheer ability to learn (great as that is) than how much and what particular sorts of things he *has* to learn in order to function at all."[8]

The dependence of the human animal on culture results from the fact that much of human evolution occurred in conjunction with the emergence of culture. "As our central nervous system – and most particularly its crowning curse and glory, the neocortex – grew up in great part in interaction with culture, it is incapable of directing our behavior or organizing our experience without the guidance provided [by culture's] systems of significant symbols." Geertz concludes that such symbols are therefore "not mere expressions, instrumentalities, or correlates of our biological, psychological, and social existence; they are prerequisites of it. Without men, no culture, certainly; but equally, and more significantly, without culture, no men" (p. 49).

The idea that our understanding of ourselves is socially conditioned has been developed by the American philosopher Richard Rorty in his *Contingency, Irony, and Solidarity*.[9] In a series of essays on the contingency of language, selfhood and community, Rorty argues that the language we speak, the community we have, and our sense of self are all contingent, products of historical events that could have been otherwise. Thus, our possibilities for self-understanding and personal identity are products of choices of certain metaphors made in earlier times, chance shifts in the uses of words, arbitrary descriptions introduced into the culture, and so on. These contingent factors work together to create an all-pervasive background understanding that informs our shared ways of speaking and doing things.

A particularly vivid example is the invention of the word "teenager" in 1941. The appearance and widespread use of this word has played a pivotal role in shaping the behavior and self-understanding of a group of people who previously had been described and treated as young adults. Once the classification "teenager" was invented, it became possible to define more clearly what is needed to keep this group from entering the labor force and competing with adults for jobs. They have come to be penned up in giant holding tanks (called "High Schools") where they wait their turn to enter the labor market and become workers. The identification of teenagers has brought with it phenomena such as juvenile delinquency, pre-teens, teeny boppers and bad teen singers. Though there have always been people in the age-bracket between thirteen and nineteen, the invention of the classification "teenager" contributed to creating a new way of being that in a straightforward sense can be called a new sort of human being.

On the view Rorty develops, once we recognize that all our possibilities of self-understanding are drawn from the pool of possibilities laid out by our historical culture, and once we see that all these possibilities are contingent, non-binding, we will see that we are free to cobble together whatever personal identity works for us. Since all criteria of goodness and coherence are products of a particular culture, as contingent as everything else, we should not feel obliged in our self-creation to measure up to any standards other than our own. Recognizing the contingency of all self-interpretations also opens the way to a stance of irony toward all self-definitions. For if I see that every self-description and self-evaluation is arbitrary, having no basis other than contingent facts about what has popped up in my culture, I will also realize that my own most basic commitments and defining ideals are ultimately up for grabs, temporary resting places on a road of self-creation that ends only with death. Rorty suggests that such a stance of irony is quite liberating. When I see myself as an ongoing event of self-creation that is answerable to no one, I can make up my own life story in any way I like, constrained only by the limits of what is on the table in my culture and my own imagination.

Michel Foucault uses social constructionism as a basis for questioning the entire notion of the subject. We saw that modernity regards the subject in a heroic light as the center of experience and action. This conception is grounded in the etymology of the word "sub-ject," meaning "that which underlies" or "is thrown under." Modern anthropocentrism treats the subject as that which grounds and provides a center for everything that exists. Foucault suggests, however, that in the contemporary world we are subjects in another sense, a sense that relies on the idea of subjection to something. "There are two meanings of the word *subject*," Foucault says, "subject to someone else by control and dependence, and tied to his own identity by a conscience or self-knowledge. Both meanings suggest a form of power which subjugates and makes subject to."[10] In his writings, Foucault tries to show that our modern understanding of ourselves as subjects of inwardness in fact subjugates us and compels us to engage in constant self-surveillance and a struggle to be "normal." Far from it being the case that being a subject is liberating and empowering, on this view, the modern understanding of the self closes off possibilities and levels life down to a lowest common denominator. It should be clear that Rorty and Foucault come up with very different conclusions from the contingency of selfhood. Where Rorty sees something liberating and positive about social constructionism, Foucault primarily focuses on the way that modern ideas produce forms of power that dominate and oppress us, forcing us into molds that keep society functioning but do little to improve our lives.

Looking at one more version of social constructionism will show the range of responses opened by the postmodern outlook. The psychologist Kenneth Gergen, in *The Saturated Self*, describes the way multiple social involvements and roles undermine the ability to experience ourselves in terms of the ideal of the self-encapsulated subject of modernity. In the place of that older experience of the self we now experience a *pastiche self* characterized by fluid boundaries and a multiplicity of actors who "come out" in various contexts. As he puts it, in contemporary life we are

bombarded with ever-increasing intensity by the images and actions of others; our range of social participation is expanding exponentially. As we absorb the views, values, and visions of others, and live out the multiple plots in which we are enmeshed, we enter a postmodern consciousness. It is a world in which we no longer have a secure sense of self, and in which doubt is increasingly placed on the very assumption of a bounded identity with palpable attributes.[11]

Bombarded, beleaguered, shoved around – this is the vocabulary postmodern theorists use to describe the way we postmodern selves are constructed by forces we can barely grasp and can never master. Our identity is something that comes to us already made by our culture. Though postmodern theorists disagree on the extent to which we are capable of remaking this ready-made thing, they agree that being a "self" is always culturally and linguistically conditioned.

The literary theorist Jonathan Culler sums up the postmodern de-centering of the subject clearly and succinctly. In postmodern theory, Culler writes, "the subject is broken down into its constituents, which turn out to be impersonal systems of convention." What constitutes the subject, according to postmodern theory, is a background of understanding laid out in advance by the discursive structures and forms of practice that inhabit a person as he or she becomes a place-holder in a public context. Culler continues:

> As it is deconstructed, broken down into component systems
> that are all transsubjective, the self or subject comes to
> appear more and more as a construct: the result of systems
> of conventions. When a man speaks, he artfully "complies
> with language;" language speaks through him, as does
> desire and society. Even the idea of personal identity
> emerges through the discourse of a culture. The "I" is not
> something given; it comes to exist, in a mirror stage which
> starts in infancy, as that which is seen and addressed
> by others.[12]

It should be obvious that this postmodern picture leaves no
room for the notion of authenticity as originally conceived.
When the self is understood as a mere side-effect of culture,
there is no way to regard the social circumstances of life as
something negative in contrast to a Real Me underlying social
roles. But even though postmodern thinkers give up on the
original conception of authenticity as a matter of being true
to a substantial Real Me, they make claim to a new ideal – a
sort of postmodern version of authenticity – that preserves
some of what the original ideal promised. This is the ideal of
clear-sightedly and courageously embracing the fact that
there is no "true self" to be, of recognizing that where we
formerly had sought a true self, there is only an empty space,
a gap or a lack. The postmodern ideal, then, is to *be* that lack of
self with playfulness and ironic amusement. A model for this
new conception of authentic existence is found in Nietzsche's
image of a "great health" in which one no longer feels any
obligation to revere what in earlier times was seen as holy or
authoritative, but instead "plays naively – that is, not delib-
erately but from overflowing power and abundance – with all
that was hitherto called holy, good, untouchable, divine."[13]

We are really true to ourselves, in other words, when we unflinchingly face the fact that there is nothing to be true to.

A common criticism of the postmodern way of de-centering the subject is that it treats the self as nothing more than a pawn in games that are being played out at the social level. What is lost here, it is said, is any sense of the self as an agent playing a part in its own life. To remedy this deficiency, some philosophers and psychologists have formulated a conception of a *dialogical self* as an alternative to both the modern monological self and the postmodern centerless self. The idea of the dialogical self, which originates in the work of the early twentieth-century Russian literary theorist, Mikhail Bakhtin, calls attention to the way that much of our ordinary experience and thought takes the form of a dialogue with real or imagined interlocutors.[14] The idea that thought is dialogical is not surprising if we consider how we first begin to use words. The child's first grasp of language is developed as a rule in scenarios that involve an interchange with parents. The child falls on her knee, for example, begins to cry, and is comforted by her mother who says, "That's not so bad." Next time she falls, she will articulate her experience in an internalized exchange with her mother: "That's not so bad," or perhaps, "No, it is bad!"[15]

There are two consequences of these language-acquiring scenarios. First, it is found that the actual experience of pain the individual has is given a determinate quality through this and similar scenarios. It is because we have internalized the idea that this kind of pain is "not so bad" that most of us learn to brush off or ignore mild forms of pain as the years go by. The fact that experience is always run through the filters of different groups' linguistic interpretations means that the qualitative experience of pain differs from one culture to another. Second, as the child matures, her thinking during the day takes the form of dialogical interchanges with imagined parental figures, teachers, friends, peers, and, later, bosses, co-workers, advisors, doctors, and other dialogical partners. For those who have a mentor or loved one in their lives, much of what they experience during the day is experienced through a lens of self-talk that is colored by an anticipation of telling the other, at the end of the day, "how things went." The conclusion to draw from the dialogical nature of experience is that we experience the world through a "We" before we experience it through an "I."[16]

According to Bakhtin's dialogical conception of human existence, we are at the deepest level *polyphonic* points of intersection with a social world rather than *monophonic* centers of self-talk and will. For this reason, we generally come to have a better knowledge of who we are through our social interactions than we do through introspection or self-reflection. The primacy of the social in defining the self has been expressed powerfully by the German philosopher Hans-Georg Gadamer, who in characterizing what it is to be human emphasizes the "between" of the interchange between conversational partners. As Gadamer says, "Long before we understand ourselves through the process of self-examination, we understand ourselves in a self-evident way in the family, society, and state in which we live. [For this reason], the focus of subjectivity is a distorting mirror. The self-awareness of the individual is only a flickering in the closed circuits of [social and] historical life."[17]

The dialogical conception of the self has the advantage of making social interactions absolutely fundamental to our identity. It lets us see that being human is inextricably being part of a "We." The psychologist Frank Richardson and his colleagues put it this way: "The mature human self is not essentially a center of monological consciousness, [where this is typically] conceived of as an inner space or mind that contains representations of things outside or inside this container self. . . . Rather, it is a scene or locus of dialogue." In this respect, the dialogical view provides a powerful corrective to the one-sided outlook of modern individualism. Instead of seeing the self as a self-encapsulated unit, a person is seen as "an interplay or conversation among various voices, commitments, identifications, or points of view."[18] At the same time, by preserving the role of the *agent* who is engaged in the dialogues, this view undercuts postmodernism's tendency to reduce the self to a mere placeholder in a web of social interactions. To be a self is to be buoyed up and carried along by social forces one can never objectify and master, but it is also to be a respondent, capable of saying "No" to some of those forces in deciding one's own life course.

The dialogical conception of the self provides a way of avoiding some of the pitfalls of modern individualism while also side-stepping the extreme displacement of the self effected by postmodern theorizing. Nevertheless, it leaves some unanswered questions. Most important is the question: *Who* precisely is this self that engages in dialogue with a variety of internalized and external voices? One proposed answer is that the self should be seen as a "dynamic multiplicity of relatively autonomous I positions in an imaginal landscape." On this view, "the I fluctuates among different and even opposed positions," responding to different "voices" that "function like interacting characters in a story."[19]

What is missing in such a picture, however, is the ability to ascribe *responsibility* to such a self. Why should any one of the multiple "I positions" feel obliged to take responsibility for any of the actions of any of the other "I positions"? If I am as many different selves as I am voices responding to different contexts, there is no "I" that can be held responsible or take responsibility for commitments undertaken across time. Like Marilyn Monroe, who is supposed to have said "Never hold me responsible for anything I said thirty minutes ago," I can dissociate myself from any obligations I undertake with no fear of feeling guilt, shame or remorse.

Richardson and his colleagues point out that a "multi-voiced self" of this sort fails because it does not take into consideration the "self-defining stand taken by individuals in the present moment concerning . . . the ends they seek" (p. 512). The idea of "taking a stand" is supposed to reinstate responsibility. The problem here, however, is that this solution to the problem also seems to reinstate the idea of the individual as the unified, self-defining center from which various responses in dialogical exchanges are made.[20] We appear to be caught in a dilemma. Either we see the self at the core of dialogical interchanges as a continuous, enduring self, in which case we resurrect the modern individual. Or we see the self as a transient "stand taken in the present moment," one stand among many, in which case we seem to come back to the disjointed, dispersed self of postmodernism.

For followers of Nietzsche and postmodern thought, this image of the self standing outside the demands of responsibility and integrity can appear exhilarating. It produces the vertigo mountaineers feel on teetering over a rocky abyss, where there are no supports and anything is possible. But it must be noted that this sense of infinite possibilities carries with it a risk of fragmentation and painful dissociation of the self as an agent in the world. Where the agent is nothing but shifting fragments, with no underlying unity, the ability to be an effective agent is undermined. The risk then is that one will either be a false self, like a chameleon changing colors to blend into its current surroundings, or one will rigidly cling to one overarching set of commitments, filtering the demands of each situation through the grid of that orientation. Of course, not everyone would agree that the condition of the multiple self is so bleak. Anthony Giddens holds that it is possible to develop a "cosmopolitan self," one that integrates elements from different settings into an urban self that "draws strength from being at home in a variety of contexts."[21] But this cosmopolitan self runs the counter-risk that in being at home everywhere, he or she is ultimately homeless, uprooted, a shadow lacking any ground on which to stand. The cosmopolitan self seems to be nothing but a new mask for the bounded masterful individual of modernity.

Jane Flax, a professor of political science and practicing psychotherapist, sees an even greater risk in the postmodern de-centering of the self. "Postmodernists intend to persuade us that we should be suspicious of a notion of the self or subjectivity," she writes.

However, I am deeply suspicious of the motives of those who would counsel such a position at the same time as women have just begun to re-member their selves and to claim an agentic subjectivity available always before only to a few privileged white men. It is possible that unconsciously, rather than share such a (revised) subjectivity with the "others," the privileged would reassure us that it was "really" oppressive to them all along.[22]

Flax goes on to suggest that there could be an even more insidious side to postmodern de-centering. "I work with people suffering from 'borderline syndrome.' In this illness the self is in painful and disabling fragments. Borderline patients lack a core self without which the registering of and pleasure in a variety [of ways] of experiencing of ourselves, others, and the outer world are simply not possible" (p. 218). What postmodern theorists may not realize is the damage that can be done by undercutting or demeaning the role of a centralized, cohesive self in dealing with such a condition. "Those who celebrate or call for a 'decentered' self seem self-deceptively naïve and unaware of the basic cohesion within themselves that makes the fragmentation of experiences something other than a terrifying slide into psychosis" (pp. 218–19).

When we look at women who are struggling for control of their lives or at people who suffer from borderline personality disorders, we may conclude that the de-centered self is a luxury only a few can afford. Indeed, the de-centered self begins to look more like a symptom of underlying pathologies than an insight into the truth about human existence. One might even argue that the recent increase in the reported cases of multiple personality disorder (currently called "disassociative identity disorder") from the mere handful reported at the turn of the twentieth century to the hundreds of thousands diagnosed in the 1990s, suggests how fragile the self in our postmodern age might be.[23]

Seven

Our attempt to find the true self beneath all social masks seems to have ended up in a maelstrom of centerlessness, dispersal and multiplicity. Postmodern thought goes beyond de-stabilizing the binary oppositions that frame the concept of authenticity; it obliterates any notion of a self whatsoever. When we look for the Real Me we are supposed to be true to, we find that, as Gertrude Stein said of the city of Oakland, "there is no there there." Starting from an attempt to find meaning and fulfillment in life by becoming authentic, we end up with a disjointed, fragmented collection of semi-selves living out episodic, stuttering, and other-directed lives.

Philosophers who are dissatisfied with the upshot of postmodernism have come to suspect that the trouble begins when we look for a substantial, fixed, enduring self that underlies the shifting desires, moods, relations, and involvements that make up a person's life. When no such self can be found, it is tempting to assume that all that we really have is a centerless swirl of transient relationships and events with nothing to hold them together. To counteract this picture, some philosophers and psychologists have proposed a way of thinking about the self not as a thing or object of any sort, but as an unfolding *story* with certain distinctive features. According to this view, the self is indeed socially constituted, as postmodern theorists claim. We all draw our concrete ways of understanding and evaluating ourselves from the pool of possible interpretations made accessible in the social context in which we find ourselves. But, at the same time, we have the ability to shape an identity for ourselves by taking over those social interpretations in our active lives and knitting them together into a unique life story.

What determines personal identity on this view, then, is not the static self-sameness of a pregiven thing through time, but the continuous, ongoing, open-ended activity of living out a story over the course of time. It is this narrative unity and continuity that defines the "I." The analogy with narrativizing suggests that, just as we impart meaning to events by telling them to ourselves and to others, so we are constantly imparting cohesiveness and coherence to our lives by enacting a life story in our actions. Seen from this standpoint, we are not just tellers of a story, nor are we something told. We are a telling.[1]

The narrativist conception of life has a number of important consequences. First, it suggests that even though we draw the materials for our life stories from the stock of roles, lifestyles and character traits available in the public world, it is up to each of us to make something of ourselves in what we do. And this means that the self is something we *do*, not something we find. We are self-making or self-fashioning beings.

Second, the narrativist view of the self emphasizes the fact that we are always embedded in and dependent on a wider, shared context of meanings we do not create ourselves. In living out our lives, each of us composes a personal identity out of the materials we find in the surrounding cultural context. Here again the analogy to telling a story holds. Just as the activity of composing a narrative draws on the language, genres and canonical stories circulating in the public world, so our own life stories must draw on the interpretations and patterns of action we come to master as we grow up into a particular culture. And just as for a story teller language is an enabling condition that opens doors to sometimes startling originality and creativity, so our access to shared ways of thinking and acting opens us up to original and creative ways of living. Our embeddedness in a social context, far from being a stultifying constraint, is what makes it possible to be innovative and creative in the first place.

A third feature of the narrativist view of the self is a specific conception of the nature of human lived time. The best way to understand this conception of temporality is by contrasting it with the standard conception of "clock time" presupposed by the sciences and so-called common sense. According to the standard view, time is simply an endless sequence of "nows" following one after the other, extending from the past through the present into the future. The past has a privileged status, according to this view, because events in the past have caused the events that are occurring in the present and will occur in the future. Though both past and future do not exist now, the future is especially unreal: it is "but a dream," something ethereal, a mere promissory note.

In contrast to the standard conception of clock time, human lived time has a richer and more complex structure. In our actual experience of our lives as agents, what has priority is the future, where the future is understood as an open realm of aims and ideals that guide us and give our actions a point. It is the open range of possibilities for the future that lets past come alive and mean something to us. We experience the past as a set of resources carried forward in achieving what we hope to accomplish. Finally, the present is experienced not as the one truly existing time, but rather as a point of intersection between future and past, the context of action in which purposes can be realized thanks to what is made accessible from the past. Lived time is linear: it is a forward-directed projection toward what is to come that carries along what has been. But it also has a circular structure insofar as there is a constant back-and-forth between the meaningful possibilities of action opened by the past and the range of goals that open up the future.

The analogy between living a story-shaped life and ordinary story telling holds up in thinking about lived time. For just as the story teller always composes his or her story on the basis of some conception of where the course of events is going overall – how it will "all come out in the end" – so life is generally lived with some sense of where things are going as a whole. There is nevertheless one important difference between the composition of works of fiction and actually living out a life story. The story teller ordinarily knows what the outcome of the story is going to be and so has considerable control over how the events will occur. In living out our lives, in contrast, we seldom know where our lives are going to go. The most we can do is envisage some range of goals and ideals and do our best to bring them to realization, leaving the rest to the contingencies of the real world.

When we see that there can be no final self-definition or closure for our life projects so long as we are still alive, the circularity built into life becomes even more apparent. In our actions, we take up the resources of the past with an eye to what we hope to achieve and at the same time we adjust our hopes and goals in the light of what befalls us. Life is therefore an open-ended and inconclusive project. We surely will die at some point. But the fact that we will die does not guarantee that <u>our lives will have a determinate meaning at the moment</u> <u>of death.</u> On the contrary, death all too often comes at an inopportune time or drags on endlessly, throwing into question the whole idea of life having a meaningful culmination. It follows, then, that the future-directedness of life does not guarantee that some end will be achieved or that the story will be wrapped up in some conclusive way. Instead, it means that in living we have a task to take up: we have the ability to organize our lives into a relatively cohesive story, a task we may assume or abandon. <u>It is up to us to determine the meaning our life stories have.</u>

Seen from the narrativist perspective, there is no substantial self beneath the ensemble of socially conditioned roles and activities that make up a life, and so there can be no such thing as getting in touch with a "real self" in order to be true to it. In other words, the notion of authenticity as traditionally conceived can get no purchase given such a view. But narrativist thinkers have formulated a conception of a way of life that is a correlate to what traditionally has been conceived as authentic. Although their conception is ultimately unsatisfying, it does a great deal to enrich our thinking about what is involved in trying to be true to oneself.

One of the most compelling versions of the narrativist notion of authenticity is encapsulated in Nietzsche's claim that you should "become what you are." The ideal of becoming what you are gains its force from the recognition that most people lead lives that are disjointed, dispersed and disowned. As we grow up to be adults, most of us evolve into individuals with a slapdash collection of traits and tendencies, and the pressures of everyday existence discourage us from forming ourselves into characters that display any real coherence and shape. In contrast to the typical way of life common to most people, Nietzsche envisions a way of living in which one comes to own and to own up to what one is. This transformed way of life is characterized in terms of " 'giving style' to one's character."[2] What is needful, Nietzsche says, is the ability to give shape to one's own self, the ability of those who "survey all the strengths and weaknesses of their nature and then fit them into an artistic plan until every one of them appears as art and reason and even weaknesses delight the eye" (GS §290). There is an image here of a constant project of self-making that involves embellishing and refining what is given in order to create a self that is truly one's own. It is important to see in this context that Nietzsche assumes that there are no antecedently given criteria for satisfactory self-formation, either within or outside oneself, no standards that determine whether one is doing a proper job of self-making. In opposition to the assumptions of the culture of authenticity, there is nothing "in me" that I need to get in touch with if I am to become what I am. Instead, the model Nietzsche has in mind is the artist who creates a distinctive work with no template or pregiven standards. To become one's own self – to "become who you are" – is to take over the task of creating oneself as a work of art.

In his commentary on Nietzsche, Alexander Nehamas describes this ideal in terms of the composition of a literary work.[3] Just as a novelist aims at integrating incidents and descriptive passages into a coherent and compelling portrayal of character and plot, so the individual strives to integrate aspects of his or her life into a cohesive character and storyline. The goal is "a continual process of greater integration of c ~'s character-traits, habits and patterns of interaction witl world" (p. 404) into an emerging story that constitutes one's self-made self. It involves imposing "a higher-order accord among one's lower-order thoughts, desires and actions" (p. 407) so that all your traits come together into a configuration you can call your own. Nehamas points out that this self-formation includes "a willingness to accept responsibility for everything that one has done, and to admit . . . that everything that one has done actually constitutes who one is" (ibid.). In other words, this way of life owns up to what is always already the case: that you *are* what you *do*, and that you can and should own up to this fact and take responsibility for what you are creating.

The ultimate goal is to create one's life as one's own story: "we want to be the poets of our life," Nietzsche says (GS §299). In composing your life story, you appropriate the actions and events that make up your life so that everything you have done "has been assembled into a whole so unified that nothing can be subtracted" without spoiling the picture.[4] In the end, your life appears as a coherent, motivated, integrated tale with no loose strands or pointless digressions. It is something you can embrace and fully own.

A somewhat different conception of authenticity is formulated by the German philosopher Martin Heidegger in his monumental work, *Being and Time*.[5] Heidegger is in agreement with narrativist thinkers generally in regarding human existence as a *life course* or *life story* stretched out between birth and death. He also agrees with social constructionists in holding that the possibilities for self-interpretation and self-evaluation we take up in living out our life stories are drawn from the social context into which we are "thrown." The social world is, on this view, the only game in town: we have nowhere to turn for roles, character ideals, lifestyles and forms of life than the social context we inhabit. Where Heidegger breaks with constructionists is in his belief that a decisive experience can counteract the tendency toward conformism endemic to social existence and transform a person's understanding of what life is all about. That experience is the confrontation with the reality of one's own death. Like Tolstoy (whose short story "The Death of Ivan Ilych" he cites as formative for his ideas), Heidegger holds that coming face to face with death can halt the tendency toward dispersal and distraction characteristic of "average everydayness" and open the possibility of living one's life as a coherent story.

To face up to death is to see your life as a finite project, something that can and will be finished. This awareness of human finitude brings with it the realization that it is up to you to determine the overall shape your life will have. Using the narrativist way of reading Heidegger developed by the French philosopher Paul Ricoeur, we can say that the recognition of life's finitude displays the distinctive structure of human lived time that defines a life course, a temporal structure that mirrors the structure of narrative time itself.[6]

Heidegger sees the confrontation with death as opening the door to an existence he calls "authentic." This conception of owning oneself is quite different from that formulated by Nietzsche. We saw that Nietzsche pictures authentic existence as an ongoing project of self-formation governed solely by such aesthetic ideals as coherence, unity, cohesiveness and style. It is seen as a playful and "naïve" mixing and matching of ideals found among the ruins of collapsed traditions. In contrast, Heidegger formulates his conception of authenticity in terms of an initial recognition of the gravity of human finitude. To see that we are finite is to see that for us not everything is possible – we are not gods – and to thereby see how important it is to take over the time allotted to us and make something of it. The German word translated as "authentic" in *Being and Time* (the word *eigentlich*) comes from a stem meaning "own" (*eigen*) and carries with it a connotation of owning oneself, owning up to what one is becoming, and taking responsibility for being one's own. To "become who you are," as Heidegger sees it, is to identify what really matters in the historical situation in which you find yourself and to take a resolute stand on pursuing those ends. Through resoluteness and commitment, life comes to have cumulativeness and directedness, and it thereby achieves a kind of lived temporal continuity Heidegger calls "constancy" and "steadfastness." Moreover, since the projects you can take over are all inherited from the historical culture into which you are thrown, to take a stand on what matters is always at the same time to be engaged in the shared undertakings (Heidegger calls it the *destiny*) of a larger community. For Heidegger, then, authenticity is found to have the sort of irreducible social dimension we will discuss in the next chapter.

The narrativist conception of the self has been developed in interesting ways in recent years by some English-speaking philosophers and psychologists. Alasdair MacIntyre in his seminal book, *After Virtue*, makes a case for thinking of "human action in general as enacted narratives."[7] The connection between action and narrative becomes evident when we note that human actions have beginnings, middles and endings much like those found in narratives. Actions can also be experienced as having genres, that is, as being tragic, comic, melodramatic, and so forth, just as narratives have genres. Moreover, like brief accounts of episodes, which only make sense in terms of their place within larger stories about agents and their settings, actions in general are identifiable and intelligible *as* actions only in terms of their place within a wider narrative or set of narratives about the agents involved and the context in which the action takes place. So, for example, a sudden jerking movement of an arm will be perceived as a mere reflex and not as an action unless it is possible to place the bit of behavior in the context of larger stories about the agent's intentions and the sorts of action that are appropriate within settings of this sort.

Based on considerations of this sort, MacIntyre draws two main conclusions. First, he claims that "we all live out narratives in our lives" (p. 212). Stories are not just tales we cook up after the fact when we tell about what happened; they are something we enact in undertaking actions of various sorts. And, second, MacIntyre points out that any individual's life story is embedded in, and only makes sense in terms of, a set of interlocking narratives as these unfold within the wider context of a historical culture. To understand a particular agent, then, is to understand how his or her life story dovetails into the stories of others, and how all these stories are related to the stories of the social settings in which various types of action make sense. This means, in MacIntyre's vocabulary, that meaningful human life must be seen as embedded in a *tradition*, where this word refers to a vital, ongoing conversation about how things count and about what is really important for a community. To say that a human agent is to be understood as a narrative, then, is to say that human existence is inescapably embedded in a wider context of meaning, a tradition, which itself has the shape of an unfolding narrative.

Drawing in part on MacIntyre's narrativist account of the self, Charles Taylor argues that to have or be a *self* is to experience one's life as an unfolding story in terms of which one can grasp what one has become and where one is going.[8] For Taylor, the experience of a life as an unfolding story is necessary to having an identity in the full sense of that word. To have an identity – to be able to answer the question, "Who are you?" – you must have an understanding of what is of crucial importance to you, and that means knowing where you stand within a context of questions about what is truly worth pursuing in life. In other words, to have an identity is to have some orientation in what Taylor calls "moral space," where the term "moral" refers to whatever gives meaning and direction to a life. As Taylor puts it,

> My identity is defined by the commitments and identifications which provide the frame or horizon within which I try to determine from case to case what is good, or valuable, or what ought to be done, or what I endorse or oppose. In other words, it is the horizon within which I am capable of taking a stand. (p. 27)

Having an orientation in a horizon of moral concerns in turn presupposes that you have some idea how you are doing in relation to those concerns, that is, that you can see where you are coming from, where you now stand, and where you still have to go to get to where you want to be. And this sense of how you are faring in the world is possible only if you experience your life as an ongoing story with identity-defining aims and an underlying direction.

Like MacIntyre, Taylor emphasizes the embedded nature of life stories. In order to be a person or agent in the full sense of those words, we must be able to respond to questions about where we stand and who we are in saying and doing the things we do. This ability to give an answer, to be *answerable* or responsible in our interchanges with others, is crucial to having an identity. It should be obvious that responsibility in this sense requires an understanding of where you stand on the fundamental issues of concern in your community. It follows that the horizon of moral questions that defines one's identity must be understood as an irreducibly public space of questions about where we stand on the issues. In Taylor's view, this embeddedness of identity in a shared context shows that the narrativist conception of the self is inseparable from the dialogical conception we examined in Chapter 5. As dialogical and story-shaped beings, we are responsible or accountable in a dual sense. First, we are able to give a response to the question of where we stand in relation to shared concerns of our community. And second, we can be counted on by others to take part in confronting the issues facing our community.[9] Where these traits are missing, Taylor claims, there is only a mutilated, partial self, one lacking any clear identity or ability to be an effective agent in the world.

Taylor's robust conception of a person or self as necessarily having a core of strong, defining commitments is also developed by the American philosopher Harry Frankfurt in his book, *The Importance of What We Care About*.[10] What is necessary to being a person in the full sense of that word, Frankfurt claims, is having "freedom of the will." To clarify what freedom of the will means, Frankfurt contrasts a full-blooded person with a human being who is not fully a person, someone he calls a *wanton*. A wanton is described as an individual who not only gives in to the pull of various cravings and whims that come over him, but furthermore does not care about what sort of will he has. An example of such a wanton would be a drug addict who fully understands his addictive behavior but does not care whether he is enslaved to his habit. Such an individual, Frankfurt claims, lacks the kind of will that is necessary to being a person.

In contrast to a wanton, a *person* is a human agent who cares about what sorts of desire motivate her to action. Such a person may be subject to the pull of various cravings and tendencies and may actually give in to these cravings and tendencies. But what makes her a person is the fact that she has second-order concerns about what sorts of first-order motivations lead her to act in the ways she does. Moreover, it is characteristic of a person that she *strongly identifies* with those second-order commitments that range over her actual first-order desires and inclinations. Her desire to exercise self-control and be free of her addiction is something she experiences as definitive of who she really is.

To be a person, then, is to be *invested* in the second-order ideals one most deeply cares about. It is to have some range of fundamental commitments that bind one's life together into a more or less cohesive whole. This is supposedly what makes persons different from animals. Although nonhuman animals may have desires and beliefs, those mental states seem to occur in a life that is merely a succession of separate moments with no overarching sense of identity to bind them together. With nothing that carries the moments of life forward in relation to commitments to the future, "there is no continuing subject," and so no self or person. What is distinctive about the life of a person, according to Frankfurt, is that the moments of life are not connected merely by formal relations of sequentiality, but are instead bound together by the overarching cares that define the identity of the person (p. 83).

Frankfurt suggests that being a person in the fullest sense requires *wholeheartedly* identifying with certain bedrock concerns and commitments that are experienced as definitive of one's identity. In the most extreme case, it is to be like Martin Luther who, when called on to recant his views, replied, "Here I stand; *I can do no other*" (p. 86). Or, to take a similar case, it is to be like Thomas More, the "man for all seasons," who stood by his religious beliefs even though he knew it meant death. Wholehearted commitments are unconditional in the sense that they are experienced as definitive of who you are. As the philosopher John Kekes says, they "define our limits: what we feel we must not do no matter what. . . . They are fundamental conditions of being ourselves."[11]

This long excursion through narrativist conceptions of the self leads us to a way of thinking of authenticity not as a matter of being true to some pregiven attributes of an antecedently given, substantial self, but instead as a matter of finding and coming to embody a set of defining commitments *that first make us into selves*. To be authentic, on this account, is to take a wholehearted stand on what is of crucial importance for you, to understand yourself as defined by the unconditional commitments you undertake, and, as much as possible, to steadfastly express those commitments in your actions throughout the course of your life. What shapes your identity, according to this picture, is determined by what you identify with: the life-defining ideals and projects that make you who you are.

The conception of authentic existence I have culled from narrativist philosophers provides a correlate to the dominant conception of authenticity without falling prey to the belief in a static, pregiven self distinct from one's actions in the world. It seems fair to say that the new account of authentic existence offered here is the legitimate heir of what used to be called "authenticity." The question still remains, however, whether this new conception of authentic existence fulfills the function of the older conception. Does it do the job that the older conception was designed to do? Does it satisfy the deep-felt human needs that the original conception tried to satisfy?

At this point we need to recall what it is that the original conception of authenticity was supposed to do. A central part of the appeal of this idea resided in the fact that it promised to give us a privileged access to something deep within ourselves that would provide us with knowledge about how we ought to live. Whether that knowledge was regarded as pertaining to a personal calling, to the voice of nature within, to the creative powers of one's own imagination, or to one's own deepest needs and capacities, the important thing was that, in being authentic, one was supposed to know something one could not know in any other way. This is implied by the idea that it is a Real Me or True Self that is accessed and known in becoming authentic. Beneath the play of appearances and illusory social demands, it seemed, we could get in touch with something real and exigent, something authoritative, something worthy of our respect and obedience.

Now it is true that the narrativist conception of authenticity we have just explored assumes there is something within me to which I do have privileged access and knowledge. I have direct knowledge of my own self-making activity, the ongoing process of seizing on possibilities of self-interpretations and making them my own through my own decisions. As knowledge of what I am doing as an agent, it seems, this knowledge could not be mistaken. But in another sense, this knowing does not provide the sort of deep truth about the self promised by the older conception of authenticity. For what the older conception promised was access to substantive information about *who I really am* and *what sort of person I ought to be*, information that was supposed to provide dependable guidelines concerning how I should conduct my life. Though social pressures and current fads may tempt me away from this truth, the truth is always supposed to be there, accessible through introspection and capable of guiding action.

It is truth of this sort that seems to be missing in the alternative conception of authentic existence we have just introduced. For insofar as reflection reveals my own self-making activity in living out my life, it also reveals that there are innumerable possible storylines and genres I can impart to my life, all of them consistent with the raw materials of my nature and the events that make up my life, but none "truer to" those givens than any others.

In order to get a clearer picture of what this problem is, we might return to Nietzsche's notion of imparting "style" to one's life. A little reflection should show that there are no set limits on the styles I can adopt in surveying "all the strengths and weaknesses of [my] nature and then fit[ting] them into an artistic plan." For one thing, there are innumerable ways I could count or identify the strengths and weaknesses I have, and, indeed, innumerable ways I could decide what *counts* as a strength or a weakness. So it does not seem that anything in my nature determines how I should go about organizing my traits and deciding on an appropriate style. The open-endedness of styles and self-creation is also evident from the fact that there are no pregiven criteria determining the appropriateness of self-imparted styles. As Nietzsche says, "In the end, when the work is finished, it becomes evident how the constraint of a single taste governed and formed everything large or small. Whether this taste was good or bad is less important than one might suppose, if only it is a single taste!" (GS §290). In other words, all that matters is that you take ownership of your life story by making it your own. When it comes to deciding what sort of style you should produce, standards of "good" and "bad" have no role to play.

More temperate narrativists have tried to show that society itself always provides constraints on how a person might provide narrative continuity to his or her life. The psychologist Jerome Bruner, for example, points out that society provides protocols and canonical stories for self-tellings, and so lays out in advance a *pacte autobiographique* that defines acceptable and unacceptable narrative constructions.[12] Because we tend to fall in step with the expectations of others about how we are to enact our life stories, the self as a rule is a *res publica*, something made in public space. But the defender of the idea of authenticity will not be pleased with this concession, for, as we have seen in discussing Rousseau, the authentic individual is supposed to reject social conformism. To be authentically myself, then, it is not enough to simply go with the flow of social protocols.

It seems, then, that the narrativist take on being a self leads to the conclusion that there are innumerable ways we might constitute ourselves in imparting a narrative shape to our lives, and that there are neither inner nor outer criteria that tell us whether our life story is truly worth living. In fact, the entire idea of owning my life begins to look suspect. Where there are no guidelines or directives for taking hold of my life, the claim that I *own* my life begins to look vacuous, nothing more than the empty tautology that my own life is my own.

The narrativist conception of authentic existence we have

been exploring can leave us with a sense of the absolute contingency of all life stories. For if *any* story can be mine, then no story is *really* mine. When we recognize the multiplicity of stories we can tell and the ultimate arbitrariness of every choice of storyline, we can begin to sense the utter groundlessness of any attempt at self-formation. There is a feeling of weightlessness here that is alluded to in the film version of Milan Kundera's novel, *The Unbearable Lightness of Being*. The lead character, Tomas, observes that life only goes around once, with no rehearsals or revisions, no standards or criteria: "It all seems so light," he says, "an outline we can never fill in or correct."

Where Tomas finds in this contingency of life a license to be playful and take nothing seriously, however, others have found in it a source of self-dissociation and alienation. A deep fissure or gap seems to open up, in this experience of our condition, between the self that makes decisions about how the story is to go and the self that is located in the physical world and is exposed to the vicissitudes of life. This gap has been captured in an especially powerful way by Sartre. For Sartre, the possibility of self-consciousness implies a distinction between the self that is engaged in conscious acts, on the one hand, and the consciousness that is the object of this conscious activity, on the other. When I adopt the first-person stance toward myself, I encounter myself as a consciousness that is fully engaged in free, creative activity, one that has the power to impart a meaning to the self and its world through its own choices. Sartre calls this self the self of "transcendence," a "being-for-itself" that is limited by nothing outside itself. The picture of the self changes, however, when I adopt a third-person stance toward myself. When I see myself as an object embedded in a world, subject to the causal forces that reign there, I see something that is finite, vulnerable and unsteady. This is the self of "facticity," a "being-in-itself" whose way of being is not much different from that of other objects in the world.

Sartre's claim is that this bifurcated self creates an unresolvable tension for our attempts to produce a stable identity for ourselves. The problem becomes apparent when we consider Sartre's example of the gambling addict who is trying to control his compulsive gambling. The gambler can pull himself back from his self-destructive behavior, make a decision to stop this sort of behavior, and resolve to avoid the gaming tables from now on. From the standpoint of his first-person perspective, this resolution is an act he performs, something he is owning up to and wholeheartedly taking responsibility for, and it has all the force of his own unconstrained free will. Since he has direct knowledge of the act of will that makes the resolution, he has immediate insight into what he is making of himself through his own choices. His will is firm, and so his identity as a self is firm. No more gambling. Period.

But it is also the case that this same person is able to adopt a third-person stance toward his own act of resolve. In doing so, he recalls that he has often made such resolutions in the past, and that each time he has done so he has given in to temptation after a couple of weeks and returned to the tables. Viewed from this standpoint, his act of will is nothing but a psychological state, one among many in a long history of decisions followed by relapses. The resolve now appears as part of his facticity rather than as an act of his transcendence. The decision shows up as an unstable, shaky thing that cannot be trusted to produce any particular course of steady action. It is an object for consciousness rather than an act of consciousness itself: "The resolution is still *me* to the extent that I realize constantly my identity with myself across the temporal flux, but it is no longer *me* – due to the fact that it has become an object for my consciousness."[13]

According to Sartre's account, the shift to the third-person perspective brings with it the recognition that my own self-making activity lacks the force to determine what I *am* in an absolute sense. But if this is the case, then it may begin to look as if the conception of authentic existence derived from the notion of self-making is something of a hoax. The claim was that through my will, and through my will alone, I could take hold of my own life and wholeheartedly identify with some set of commitments that will define my identity. There was the promise here of wholeness, continuity, coherence, constancy, purposiveness and responsibility for self – qualities definitive of this new conception of an authentic existence.

But now the whole business begins to look like a set-up for disappointment. The assurance that I could take charge of my own life appears illusory when I acknowledge the fact that my self-making activity and identifications, far from creating a rock that will withstand the tests of time, are actually nothing but transient psychological episodes, as prone to pass away as any of my other psychological episodes. In the light of such a discouraging picture, one might conclude that even if such heroic individuals as Thomas More and Martin Luther could take charge of their lives through an act of sheer will, for us lesser folk such an ideal is too much to ask.

Eight

As we come to the end of our tour through different ways of thinking about authenticity, it is time to draw some conclusions about what we have found. The project of being authentic, as we have interpreted it, involves two main components. First, there is the task of pulling yourself back from your entanglements in social game-playing and going with the flow so that you can get in touch with your real, innermost self. This task requires intensive inward-turning, whether such self-inspection is called "introspection," "self-reflection," or "meditation." The assumption underlying the first component of the project of being authentic is that there is a substantial self lying deep within each of us, a self with attributes that are both distinctively our own and profoundly important as guides for how we ought to live. The second component of the project of authenticity involves living in such a way that in all your actions you express the true self you discovered through the process of inward-turning. The assumption here is that there is something fundamentally false or dishonest about social life, and for that reason it is crucially important to know who you are and *be* the person you are in all you do.

Most of the last three chapters have been devoted to questioning the assumptions underlying the first component of the project of authenticity. Chapter 5 questioned the assumption that what lies within is necessarily something good and valuable, something worth accessing and expressing in our lives. Chapter 6 considered questions about whether it makes sense to assume that there is, lying within us, a substantial self that is distinguishable from the socially constituted self. And Chapter 7 suggested that the most we can find within ourselves is a mixed bag of psychological episodes and states that are for the most part transient and not particularly dependable as guides to what we ought to do. At the end of this process of critical reflection on the notion of the authentic inner self, it has come to appear that mucking around inside the mental container, far from leading us to a better, richer life, might be a path to confusion and despair.

One might object, however, that though these criticisms show some problems in the notion of authentic existence, they do not show adequate appreciation for the fact that there is obviously something *right* about the project of being authentic. In order to bring to light what I think is right about this ideal, I want to take a closer look at the second component of the ideal of authenticity, the injunction to "be yourself" or "be true to who you are" in what you do. What exactly does this mean? As I hope to show, it turns out to mean something quite different from what our Romantic heritage has led us to think it means.

In previous chapters we noted some of the risks involved in taking authenticity as a guiding ideal for one's life. There is the risk of slipping into a life so prone to self-absorption and compulsive self-surveillance that one becomes isolated from all but those who share this preoccupation. There is the danger of bull-headed adherence to feelings and beliefs whose sole justification is that one finds through introspection that one feels that way or happens to hold these beliefs. There is the risk of being so carried away by feelings and perceived needs that one turns to actions that are either foolish or monstrous. There is the risk of falling prey to self-help gurus and pop therapists who promise "simple" answers to complex questions under the guise of showing you how to express your own authentic needs. And there is the risk of wasting your time undertaking a project of self-discovery and self-fulfillment that may be hopelessly self-defeating, a recipe for failure and disappointment.

Given the dangers involved in the project of authenticity, we might ask why we suppose that authenticity is a good thing. Why should anyone even want to be authentic? The first temptation is to see this question as absurd, like asking, Why should anyone ever want to be happy? But unlike happiness, authenticity is not a condition that is obviously good in itself. Most people would agree, I think, that becoming and being authentic is an arduous process, and that authentic people are not necessarily the happiest people in the sense of having pleasurable feelings most of the time. The ideal of authenticity makes a very heavy demand on you, one that outweighs concerns about sustaining good feelings in all situations. To see this, imagine what you would do if a drug were invented that would provide you with nothing but pleasurable feelings for the rest of your life, but would make you a mindless slave to society's conventions. Would you be willing to take that drug for the rest of your life? If you even hesitate to say "yes," then you probably feel that there is (or might be) something worthwhile about being authentic that goes beyond whatever good feelings it might bring. The question now is: What is the up side of authenticity? What is its appeal?

I think that most of us are inclined to see authenticity as an ideal character trait or personal virtue that is necessary to living the best possible life for humans under modern circumstances. The philosopher Charles Taylor has clarified this idea in *The Ethics of Authenticity*. In earlier, premodern societies, Taylor points out, people as a rule found their identity through coming to understand their place within the context of society and the wider cosmic order. Finding one's place in such a context provided the individual with a sense of what is worth pursuing in life, and it gave people a basis for seeing what they ought to do and for assessing how they were doing. The familiar model for such a view is the old idea of "my station and its duties." As we saw in Chapter 2, for people in premodern societies the central concern was with honor, that is, with doing well in the performance of one's socially prescribed roles. It follows that, in such societies, the primary orientation of life was "outward" rather than inward: what mattered was how one was faring in the shared undertakings of communal life.

With the rise of the modern worldview, the older context for determining how one should act has been replaced with an outlook in which individual responsibility and the choice of careers has become fundamental. In the modern world, one finds one's path through life not by getting clear about the circumstances of one's birth or one's station in life, but through discovering the options that are available in the world, getting clear about one's own desires, interests and talents, and choosing a path in the light of one's own deepest desires and needs. For this approach to life, what is important is not "doing what one does," not going with the flow, but knowing what you want and having the ability to chart your own course. The central issue for modernity is *autonomy*, self-direction, being the captain of your own ship. What we hope to achieve in life is not honor as that was traditionally conceived, but rather the *dignity* that arises from being a bounded, masterful, autonomous self. For the modern outlook, your sense of self-worth is based on the dignity of being a self-directed, effective actor in the world.

The modern picture of agency shows us why authenticity seems to be such a central concern for living a good life. Being self-directed requires (1) knowing what you believe and feel and (2) honestly expressing those beliefs and feelings in what you do. For this purpose, it is less important *what* you believe and feel than *how* deep those feelings and beliefs are. The modern picture of the ideal person is a picture of an independent, self-directed individual whose actions clearly manifest what he or she really is. It is an image of a focused, effective agent interacting with others and participating in public affairs with a degree of clarity, courage and integrity normally lacking in inauthentic individuals.

What we need to notice in this way of characterizing authentic existence is that the role of authenticity as described here has at its core a motivation that is more social than it is personal. In the language of virtues, we might say that authenticity is assumed to be a virtue more concerned with the individual's personal fulfillment, rather like temperance, than it is a social virtue comparable to fairness and decency. The conception of authenticity as a personal matter follows from Lionel Trilling's distinction between sincerity and authenticity. Where the former is clearly a social concern, the latter is understood to be entirely a personal issue. That is why authenticity involves such a disparaging attitude toward the social circumstances of life: worrying about fitting in and being a well-adapted member of society is the definition of inauthenticity. A number of the thinkers we have discussed put a great deal of emphasis on the social dimension of authentic existence. This is especially true of Heidegger, Taylor and Bruner, but it is also true of Sartre and de Beauvoir. And, as we saw at the outset of this study, Oprah, Dr. Phil and other self-help writers always emphasize the importance of our relations to others. But the heart of most conceptions of authenticity tends to be the personal concern with achieving self-realization and personal fulfillment through getting in touch with one's own inner self.

In this final chapter, I want to explore the idea that the problems running through the standard idea of authenticity result from thinking of it solely as a personal virtue. What I will propose is that we think of authenticity as being fundamentally and irreducibly a social virtue. What would authenticity as a social virtue look like?

In recent years, two especially insightful philosophers have tried to articulate a conception of authenticity (and its related ideal, integrity) as a social virtue. The first of these, the late Bernard Williams, presents an extremely subtle and thoughtful reflection on the notion of authenticity in a chapter entitled "From Sincerity to Authenticity" in his book, *Truth and Truthfulness*.[1] As the title of this chapter suggests, Williams starts out from Lionel Trilling's *Sincerity and Authenticity*, and like Trilling, he makes Rousseau a pivotal figure in his story. As we saw earlier, Rousseau is committed to the belief that if he truthfully expresses what he feels at any moment, he is assured of being authentic in the sense of "being himself." The crucial concern for Rousseau is being true to the inner self as it reveals itself and expressing it openly, with full candor, and without any embellishing or editing. Through this sort of authentic self-manifestation Rousseau hopes to enable others to recognize him as he truly is: he is confident that sincere, spontaneous self-expression, based solely on what is immediately presented to the self in its inwardness, will make manifest his true motives and will thereby reveal his true self, the "whole person," in a way that is coherent and steady.[2] The assumption is that even though such self-revelation reveals conflicting moods and passing feelings, in the end the true self, the underlying source for all avowals and inner states, will become manifest to others.

Williams' criticism of Rousseau's project of self-revelation begins by noting that what we express at any moment can only be an expression of what we are feeling or thinking at that moment. It is the nature of psychological events and states that they come and go. If Rousseau hopes to make manifest his true, enduring self, then, he will need to find a way to steady the flow of feelings, desires and identifications that parade by within him. How is such steadying achieved? It is often assumed that steadiness is achieved through a wholehearted identification with some core projects, traits of character or ideals. The picture here is of an intense resolution to steadfastly embrace some set of character traits as definitive of one's self. But, as we have seen, Sartre points out that dramatic psychological occurrences of this sort are just psychological occurrences, ultimately as transient and prone to break down as any other mental episodes and states. So it seems that what steadies and stabilizes the inner life cannot itself be something within the inner life, any more than what holds the beads on a necklace together can itself be just another bead.

Williams' answer to this question is that the steadiness of the inner life can be achieved only through our interactions with others within the social context in which we find ourselves. To back up this suggestion, he considers the case of a person whose declarations and expressions are all completely sincere, but whose mental constitution is so changeable that he or she has different beliefs and attitudes from one time to the next. If these beliefs and stances changed too often, Williams says, we would not be able to see them as beliefs and identifications at all. This is the case because attributing beliefs and attitudes to someone requires that we see them to be fairly steady. For this reason, our expressions of belief and attitude need to form a pattern for them to even *count* as avowals of belief or opinion. In the same way, if someone is too capricious and unpredictable, it becomes questionable whether they have a self to be "true to" at all.

It may be the case, of course, that there are people who as a matter of fact always feel and believe the same things. For them, the pattern characterizing their inner life and defining the self is unavoidably presented in their truthful expressions. But for most of us, the fact that we have dynamic mental constitutions makes it likely that our views and feelings are subject to change as we confront different situations. So the question arises again: How is the continuity and coherence of the self possible? How do our beliefs and attitudes come to have enough of a pattern for them to present themselves *as* the beliefs and attitudes of a self at all?

Williams' answer to these questions is in agreement with the view of the dialogical self discussed in Chapter 6. According to Williams, the requisite steadiness and patterning in our beliefs and feelings are made possible by our social interactions. In the course of dealing with others, we are expected to have some degree of consistency in our avowals and expressions over time. What makes such consistency possible is a set of social practices that more or less gently nudge people into being steady in the responses elicited by others and, eventually, by themselves. We can say that someone is "way out of line" because we live in a world where keeping people in line and making them responsible for keeping in line are givens. As we grow up into this shared world, we "learn to present ourselves to others, and consequently to ourselves, as people who have moderately steady outlooks or beliefs" (p. 192). Confronted with a novel sort of situation and asked what we believe or how we feel, we may simply blurt out some spontaneous response. But having given that response, social pressures lead us to either own up to it and hold to it in a steady way, or to retract it and align ourselves with some other response.

The important thing to see here is that being a self that holds beliefs and honestly expresses those beliefs is made possible not by our having direct access to our inner lives, but by the processes of socialization and cultivation that transform us from chaotic, childish bundles of transient response into mature adults with fairly well-formed, stable selves. The conclusion Williams draws is that "we must leave behind the assumption that we first and immediately have a transparent self-understanding," and recognize that "we are all together in the social activity of mutually stabilizing our declarations and moods and impulses into becoming such things as beliefs and relatively steady attitudes" (p. 193).

Note that Williams is not simply restating the postmodern chestnut that our selves are socially constructed. He is fully aware that there is something there "inside us" both before and after society does its work. Instead, his claim is that what we call our *authentic self*, the self we access and express when we are being authentic, is at its deepest level something shaped and defined by society. Even introspection and truth-fulness are made possible by social practices, as is our very idea of ourselves as individuals. The lesson is, Williams says, that "we need each other in order to be anybody" (p. 200). It is only through our social interactions that we become selves whose inner episodes are given enough steadiness and cohesiveness so that our relations to others can be built on cooperation and trust.

This picture of the social context of authenticity transforms our sense of what is involved in being authentic. Authenticity requires something more than making a decision to identify with something, where *what* we identify with is irrelevant so long as we do it with enough intensity and passion. Instead, we need to see that our identity-conferring identifications are drawn from, and are answerable to, the shared historical commitments and ideals that make up our communal life-world.[3] What imparts authoritative force to our decisions and commitments is not the wholeheartedness of the commit-ment, important as that may be, but rather the authority of the cultural traditions and social practices that form the shared background of intelligibility for our beliefs, commit-ments, feelings and decisions. Seen from this point of view, becoming an authentic individual is not a matter of recoiling from society in order to find and express the inner self. What it involves is the ability to be a reflective individual who discerns what is genuinely worth pursuing within the social context in which he or she is situated.

In her essay, "Standing for Something," Cheshire Calhoun examines a concept closely related to authenticity, the notion of integrity.[4] The character ideal of integrity is commonly understood as involving an ability to form an integrated self through wholehearted commitments, that is, through standing for something. Having firm and enduring commitments of this sort is supposed to shape a person's character and thereby provide the person with a stable identity. Having such a character and identity, it is assumed, is what is needed to be able to genuinely believe in something and so to act on principle when faced with difficult choices.

Calhoun raises the question whether integrity should be understood as a personal or a social virtue. As she notes, personal virtues are those that are solely conducive to the well-being of the individual – the traditional example is temperance, a virtue that serves primarily to help the individual maintain health and psychological balance. Personal virtues are distinguished from social virtues, for example, charity or justice, virtues whose primary role is to enable us to conduct ourselves properly in our dealings with others. In addition to virtues that are overwhelmingly personal or social, there are also virtues that are both personal and social – for example, self-respect, a virtue that is conducive both to a proper regard for one's own moral status and also for attaining proper regard among others in a community. Calhoun suggests that most people assume that integrity is entirely a personal virtue: its value is seen as lying in the fact that it enriches and reinforces the individual's identity, integration of characteristics, and ability to take a stand. In opposition to this common view, Calhoun tries to show that integrity should be seen as both a personal and a social virtue.

We might try to apply Calhoun's line of reasoning to the concept of authenticity, asking whether it should be understood as a personal virtue, a social virtue, or as both. We saw at the outset that Trilling's way of contrasting sincerity and authenticity makes authenticity look like a purely personal matter. In contrast to sincerity, which aims at ensuring truthfulness in our relations to others, authenticity has as its sole aim achieving truthfulness with respect to oneself. Seen from this standpoint, we tend to suppose that people who worry about others, the "people-pleasers" and "codependents," lie at the opposite pole from authenticity. Thinking about others is seen as bad faith, a failure of nerve in our project of being true to ourselves. Authenticity properly understood, it is assumed, has nothing to do with social relations.

It might be the case, however, that authenticity looks like a purely personal project only because of the way it is generally understood. The common view of the authentic individual, we have seen, is of a person who knows how she feels about things and expresses those feelings in all her actions. What I want to question is whether this description by itself really captures everything we expect from the notion of authenticity. To approach the question, we might try to imagine cases of people who are authentic according to this definition but who do not really seem to be what we have in mind when we think of an authentic person. Consider, for example, someone with an unconditional commitment to making a lot of money by producing slick, popularized paintings. In imagining this case, we should suppose that the person we are imagining has great artistic talent and skill, but nevertheless dedicates his life to pumping out the kind of sentimental schlock that sells. Or imagine someone whose deepest commitment in life is enthusiastically and unquestioningly supporting whoever happens to have political power at any time, or someone whose defining life-goal is to always fit in and be as much like everyone else as possible.[5]

In each of these cases, we are imagining people who have

deep feelings about something and who express these feelings in their actions. But in each case, the commitment is to something that is either trivial or obviously compromised in some way. On the surface, at least, it seems that these people would satisfy the definition of "authenticity." But would we regard such people as being authentic? Would we attribute to them the dignity we associate with the notion of authenticity? The fact that we hesitate to apply the term "authentic" in these cases indicates that what is crucial about authenticity is not just the intensity of the commitment and fervor of the expression it carries with it, but the nature of the content of the commitment as well. In other words, for a commitment to count as authentic, it is not enough that someone feels strongly about the commitment or firmly believes that undertaking it is worthwhile. For the stance to count as authentic, there must be a way for us to see how a person might have reasons to think that such an undertaking really is worthwhile at some level.

It is no doubt because there is a conceptual connection between authenticity and having a commitment to something worthwhile that the earliest notions of authenticity presupposed that those who engage in serious introspection have access to a deeper insight into the True and the Good than those adrift in unreflective role-playing. It is also because we assume that authentic self-reflection might lead to worthy insights that we see dignity attaching to the project of being authentic. It was only when doubts began to arise about the existence of a privileged truth lying within the individual self that the notion of authenticity lost its original connection to the idea of gaining access to an authoritative source of wisdom. When the older idea of privileged access to a higher truth is abandoned, as it is in our contemporary thinking, what is left is a glorification of intensity and "mineness" as goods in themselves, no matter what their content might be. We are then inclined to think of authenticity as a purely personal virtue, one aimed at firming up the boundaries of one's own self or at strengthening one's powers of self-assertion or at affirming one's own worth as an individual or at some other purely personal end.

I want to suggest that this contemporary picture of authenticity is incoherent. To see why this is so, we might examine a case of a person we would regard as inauthentic − for example, someone who is oblivious to what she really feels and believes and who wouldn't stand up for herself even if she did know what she feels. When we consider such a case, it is obvious we have a negative and disapproving reaction to such people. We regard them as shallow, empty, gutless. We might now ask ourselves, What exactly is it we see as bad in inauthentic people?

The only answer, I think, is that they are betraying something. But what exactly are they betraying? Are they just betraying themselves, like the person who lacks moderation and overeats? It seems that the person who is inauthentic is not just betraying herself, but is betraying something we regard as essential to all of us. We feel that the inauthentic person is letting us all down. This sense of betrayal arises because we understand that a society of the type we have − a democratic society − is able to thrive only if it is made up of people who use their best judgment and discernment to identify what to them is truly worth pursuing and are willing to stand for what they believe in. When someone fails to deliberate about what is important or comes up with transparently trivial or pointless commitments, or when someone refuses to stand for what he believes, we feel that they are not doing their part to sustain a social system that depends on people who do precisely these things.

What is it about our society that makes us think that inauthentic people are letting us down? Cheshire Calhoun provides an answer in her discussion of integrity. As she observes, political theorists since John Stuart Mill have argued that a viable free and democratic society is possible only if there is a populace committed to discovering the truth through the unrestricted exchange of ideas. That is why freedom of thought and freedom of speech are essential to a free society. But freedom itself is only meaningful and effective if certain other conditions are satisfied within the society. There must be an educational system that ensures that people are knowledgeable about the issues that confront their society. There must be freedom of information so that people can be informed about what is going on. But it is also necessary for people to cultivate the character traits of honesty, courage and integrity for them to be able to deliberate carefully about what is at stake in the world and to stand up for what, in their own best judgment, is right. And, insofar as each person must start out from his or her own best judgment about how we should undertake common projects and conduct our lives together, there is a need for people to get clear about what their own deliberations lead them to believe and to honestly and fully express what they conclude in public space. This demand for honest self-expression is especially important when the ideas run against the grain of popular opinion. The expression of unpopular views is especially important for a democratic society, because it is a presupposition of a free society that it is only by playing off a diverse range of views in the ongoing conversation of the community that the best possible answers can be reached.

What these observations suggest is that one crucial reason why we value authenticity is because we believe that being authentic plays a fundamental role in nurturing and sustaining the kind of society in which something like authenticity as an ideal can be possible. The ideal of authenticity and the modern ideal of a free society are inextricably linked. If this is the case, however, then it seems clear that authenticity cannot be thought of simply as a personal virtue. It is also fundamentally a *social* virtue, one of a group of character traits that play a key role in fitting us for membership in a society of a particular sort.

This expanded conception of authenticity makes it possible to answer the charge that people who strive to be authentic are inevitably self-absorbed and self-centered. For if authenticity is essentially a social virtue, then the authentic person must have a valuable role to play in society. But authenticity will play this positive role only if it is understood in a way that parts company with some of the assumptions built into current thinking about authentic existence. To make sense of the social role of authenticity, we need to see that becoming authentic involves becoming more clear-sighted and reflective about the issues that face us in our current situation. These include questions about the kinds of relationships that will foster and strengthen a free society, the kinds of obligations we have to fulfill in order to qualify for citizenship in that society, and the kinds of global relationships we need to develop in order to increase the prospects of freedom throughout the world.[6]

Authenticity is also a social virtue in another sense. It would seem that authenticity as a way of life should carry with it the awareness that one's own ability to realize this ideal character trait is only possible within a society of a specific type. Personal projects such as being authentic or achieving dignity can be undertaken only in a world that recognizes individual talents, respects differences, provides equal opportunity, acknowledges the value of criticism and unpopular ideas, and ensures that there are no obstacles to freedom of expression. Moreover, being authentic involves more than just the awareness that a particular sort of society is needed. To be fully authentic is to recognize the need to be constantly vigilant in one's society, to be engaged in political action aimed at preserving and reinforcing a way of life that allows for such worthy personal life projects as that of authenticity. If this is the case, however, then the authentic individual cannot be thought of as someone who is simply reflective and candid in acting in the world. Such a person must also be attentive to what is going on in the political arena and politically active at all levels of society. It is through this sort of attentiveness and activism that the authentic person takes a stand not just on his or her own life, but on the community's project of achieving a good society.[7]

In the first chapter of this book, I distinguished two basic orientations open to us in trying to achieve a good life: living according to an ideal of *self-possession* or *enownment*, on the one hand, and living according to the ideal of *self-loss* or *releasement*, on the other. The project of being an authentic individual, like the character ideal of integrity, is clearly an example of what I have called "enownment." Becoming authentic, as it is commonly understood, involves centering in on your own inner self, getting in touch with your feelings, desires and beliefs, and expressing those feelings, desires and beliefs in all you do. So understood, authenticity clearly counts as a personal virtue: it aims at defining and realizing your own identity as a person. The emphasis is entirely on owning and owning up to what you are at the deepest level. The common objection that such an ideal can lead to self-absorption and an almost solipsistic concentration on one's own psychological life gains its plausibility from its extreme emphasis on self-possession.

What I have tried to suggest in this chapter is the need to bring to light the social embodiment of authenticity, the kind of role it plays in the concrete social context in which it has emerged. Although it is natural to think of authenticity as a very private and personal undertaking, a closer examination of the role of this idea in our current cultural context reveals that it makes sense only in terms of very specific social commitments. The project of authenticity as a personal undertaking is made possible by a social world in which certain sorts of democratic ideals have emerged, and it impacts on that social world in concrete ways. My suggestion has been that, when the ideal of authenticity is understood in terms of its actual social embodiment, it is clear that being authentic is not just a matter of concentrating on one's own self, but also involves deliberation about how one's commitments make a contribution to the good of the public world in which one is a participant. So authenticity is a personal undertaking insofar as it entails personal integrity and responsibility for self. But it also has a social dimension insofar as it brings with it a sense of belongingness and indebtedness to the wider social context that makes it possible. This social dimension of authenticity explains why proponents of the culture of authenticity, and especially Oprah and Dr. Phil, are so concerned about the quality of our involvements with others. Commitments to family, friends and the wider society are not just afterthoughts tacked on to a project that otherwise requires total self-preoccupation. They are integral to the very idea of authenticity as a way of life.

Bringing to light the social dimension of authenticity also suggests that the opposition between the basic life-orientations of enownment and releasement is an over-simplification. It turns out that what is at stake for achieving the most fulfilling and meaningful life is not making a choice when faced with an "either/or:" *either* you focus on self-realization *or* you lose yourself in worldly involvements. Instead, it seems that a well-lived life must somehow combine both these orientations. Self-possession is necessary in the modern world, because it is important to know how you feel about things and to candidly express your views. For this purpose, a practice of self-reflection and responsible expression is crucially important. But, as we have seen, such a practice serves its proper social role only when it provides the basis for an open and respectful exchange of views with others about issues that matter to the wider community.

The conception of an open and free conversation with others suggests that it is important sometimes to be able to release ourselves from our personal concerns and give ourselves over to the flow of something that is experienced as greater than ourselves. Such a picture of self-release in the flow of a serious conversation has been developed by a philosopher referred to earlier, Hans-Georg Gadamer. In his description of authentic conversation, Gadamer shows how the participants in the conversation can leave behind their self-preoccupations as they give themselves over to the to-and-fro of the discussion. What becomes central in a dialogical situation of this sort is not the opinion of this person or that person, but rather the *subject matter* under discussion. We all have experienced conversations in which we get so involved in the topic being discussed that we seem to become totally absorbed in the discussion. The center and focus of an intense conversation is defined by the ongoing play of ideas as they carry the matter at hand forward. The locus of the activity as we experience it is not my mind and yours, but rather the "between" made concrete in the issue of the truth of the matter we are discussing. In vital, intense discussions, egos fall away and are replaced by something much more important: the matter that matters. Gadamer describes this experience in terms of what he calls "total mediation."[8] The "being" of such a conversational context is best seen not as consisting of subjects and objects that happen to be causally interrelated at the moment, but in terms of an unfolding *event* through which people and the matters at hand come to have the concrete identity they have. In dialogical events of this sort, what is at stake is not standing up for one's own position or beating out one's opponent, but merging distinct horizons of understanding in order to reach an agreement about the truth of something that matters.

Gadamer's account of authentic conversation provides a model of what I have called self-loss or releasement, and it therefore offers a counterpoint to what can start to look like obsessive self-preoccupation and self-indulgence encouraged by self-help programs. This sort of releasement means no longer putting ourselves at the center of the picture, no longer letting our egos get in the way in every situation. It points to a way of getting into the swim of what is going on around us without asking where we stand in it all.

Heidegger in his later writings referred to this orientation toward life with the German word *Gelassenheit*, a word coming from a stem meaning "let" and suggesting "letting be," "letting go," or, as the English translation has it, "releasement."[9]

Heidegger was highly critical of the contemporary tendency to try to control everything through our own will, the desire to make everything measure up to our expectations and to make things come out in the way we want. At the level of social action, he claims, this self-assertiveness has led to the omnipresence of technology and instrumental control at every level of life. At the personal level, it leads to a preoccupation with selfish acquisitiveness and means/ends calculative thinking that generates social friction and an inability to be clear about goals. The preoccupation with control means the imposition of human will onto everything in the world, even onto our relations and our own selves. Seen from the standpoint of the quest for total control, nature presents itself as material resources on hand to be manipulated and mastered, and humans come to see even themselves as "human resources" to be used for the achievement of ever greater control. Paradoxically, self-help and human potential movements, far from providing an alternative to this regime of total control, reinforce the faith in control by pressuring individuals to take control of their own lives through self-inspection, self-surveillance and self-assertion. We are even encouraged to get spirituality under control through means/ends strategies!

The notion of releasement is introduced as an alternative to this endless cycle of control. It proposes that we put aside our constant preoccupation with self-aggrandizement and machination. Instead of encouraging us to master every situation, it envisions a way of letting go of our own personal agendas and experiencing ourselves as participants in a shared event that is greater than ourselves. In this orientation to life, we focus not on what we can get out of a situation, but rather on what we can contribute to the situation. The metaphors that come naturally here are "going with the flow" and "being part of." The idea of releasement proposes not passive quietism in which one does nothing, but an activism that operates with a heightened sensitivity to what is called for by the entire situation. It is a stance that is motivated less by a concern with making than with finding, less by calling forth than being called. In place of the emphasis on calculation and insistence on one's own ends, there is the kind of situational awareness of what should be done that comes readily to those who have cultivated in themselves a sense of decency and compassion.

In introducing the idea of releasement, I am not suggesting we should turn ourselves into mindless robots or become doormats who put up with whatever anyone does to us. On the contrary, I have tried to show that the ideal of authenticity, when properly understood, has a valuable role to play in our lives. But I am trying to call attention to the dangerous one-sidedness built into the concentration on authenticity that can arise in certain areas of the self-help movement. What is problematic is not the idea of authenticity, but a narrow and obsessive concern with that ideal at the expense of other valuable ideals and orientations open to us in life. What is problematic, as I see it, is not the goal of being authentic, but the predominance of any one perspective on the rich and dense weave of undertakings and responsibilities that make up our lives.

Notes

PREFACE

1 See, for example, the essays in Mark Wrathall and Jeff Malpas, eds., *Heidegger, Authenticity, and Modernity: Essays in Honor of Hubert L. Dreyfus*, vol. 1 (Cambridge, MA: MIT Press, 2000), or my own essays, "Becoming a Self: The Role of the Concept of Authenticity in *Being and Time*," in C. Guignon, ed., *The Existentialists* (Lanham, MD.: Rowman & Littlefield, 2003), pp. 119–32, and "Authenticity, Moral Values, and Psychotherapy," in C. Guignon, ed., *The Cambridge Companion to Heidegger* (Cambridge: Cambridge University Press, 1993), pp. 215–39. The German language has a word traditionally used by philosophers to refer to what we call authenticity: it is *Authentizität*. The word Heidegger uses, *Eigentlichkeit*, would sound strange to the German ear, and translating it as "authenticity" would sound even stranger. I owe this bit of information to Frank-M. Staemmler.

2 Stuart Jeffries, "Bernard Williams: The Quest for Truth," *The Guardian*, November 30, 2002, online p. 4.

3 Stanley Cavell, *Conditions Handsome and Unhandsome: The Constitution of Emersonian Perfectionism* (LaSalle, IL: Open Court, 1990), p. 18.

4 Russell B. Goodman, "Moral Perfectionism and Democracy: Emerson, Nietzsche, Cavell," *Emerson Society Quarterly*, 43 (1997): 159–80, p. 164.

5 Ibid., p. 166; the quote is from Ralph Waldo Emerson, *The Collected Works of Ralph Waldo Emerson* (Cambridge, MA: Belknap Press, 1971), 2: 30.

6 Tom Wolfe, "The Me Decade and the Third Great Awakening," in his *Mauve Gloves & Madmen, Clutter & Vine and Other Stories, Sketches, and Essays* (New York: Bantam Books, 1976), pp. 111–47.

7 Quoted in Aldous Huxley, *The Perennial Philosophy* (New York: Harper & Brothers, 1944), p. 2.

8 Charles Taylor, *Sources of the Self: The Making of the Modern Identity* (Cambridge, MA: Harvard University Press, 1989), esp. Part III.

9 Phillip C. McGraw, *Self Matters: Creating Your Life from the Inside Out* (New York: Simon & Schuster, 2001), p. 63.

10 These quotes are taken from *Oprah Winfrey Speaks: Insight from the World's Most Influential Voice* and *The Uncommon Wisdom of Oprah Winfrey*, as cited in Eric Duggan's "Oprah Fans Trust in Transformation," *St. Petersburg Times*, June 21, 2003, p. 15A.

11 L. Gregory Jones notes that no ancient language contained a word translatable as "spirituality" until the fifth century (when it meant "those who live in the Spirit"), and that the word, with its contrast to materiality, was not commonly used until the end of the Middle Ages. In the early modern era, it was used pejoratively to attack enthusiastic or quietist movements. Today it is used mainly to draw a contrast to material life. What this history of the word shows is that any attempt to talk about spirituality across cultural or historical lines is problematic, since it is unclear what conceptual boundaries the term is supposed to mark. See Jones, "A Thirst for God or Consumer Spirituality? Cultivating Disciplined Practices of Being Engaged by God," in L. Gregory Jones and James J. Buckley, eds., *Spirituality and Social Embodiment* (Oxford: Blackwell, 1997), 3–28, p. 26 n. 4.

12 Charles Taylor, *The Ethics of Authenticity* (Cambridge, MA: Harvard University Press, 1991).

ONE THE CULTURE OF AUTHENTICITY

1 A member of the audience at a taping of the new *Doctor Phil* show surely spoke for many of Oprah's fans when she said, "I'm a member of the Church of Oprah and Dr. Phil is my higher power" (*Newsweek*, September 2, 2002, p. 56).

2 McGraw, *Self Matters*, pp. 6–7, 306.

3 David Riesman, *The Lonely Crowd: A Study of Changing American Character* (New Haven: Yale University Press, 1950).

4 Norman Vincent Peale, *The Power of Positive Thinking* (New York: Prentice-Hall, 1952), p. 17.

5 Fritz Perls, "Four Lectures," in J. Fagan and I. L. Shepherd, eds., *Gestalt Therapy Now* (New York: Harper Colophon, 1970), pp. 20, 22.

6 They Might Be Giants, "Whistling in the Dark," on the album *Flood*, Live!! *New York City*, October 14, 1994.

7 Jean-Paul Sartre, *Being and Nothingness*, trans. Hazel Barnes (New York: Philosophical Library, 1956), p. 59.

8 Deepak Chopra, *The Seven Spiritual Laws of Success: A Practical Guide to the Fulfillment of Your Dreams* (San Rafael, CA: New World Library, 1994), pp. 95, 97.

9 I have examined Dostoevsky's views in my editor's introduction to *The Grand Inquisitor, with Related Chapters from "The Brothers Karamazov"* (Indianapolis: Hackett, 1993), pp. xxxvi–xliii.

10 Philip Cushman, *Constructing the Self, Constructing America: A Cultural History of Psychotherapy* (Reading, MA: Addison-Wesley, 1995), p. 244.

TWO THE ENCHANTED GARDEN

1 See especially Alexander Nehamas' *The Art of Living: Socratic Reflections from Plato to Foucault* (Berkeley: University of California Press, 2000).

2 Plato, *Republic*, trans. G. M. A. Grube, rev. by C. D. C. Reeve (Indianapolis: Hackett, 1992).

3 *The Dialogues of Plato*, vol. 2, ed. and trans. B. Jowitt (New York: Random House, 1937), p. 645.

4 M. H. Abrams, *Natural Supernaturalism: Tradition and Revolution in Romantic Literature* (New York: W. W. Norton, 1971), p. 83.

5 Augustine, *Confessions*, trans. F. J. Sheed (Indianapolis: Hackett, 1993), cited by book and chapter. This quote is from x. viii.

6 *De vera Religione*, xxxix. 72, quoted in Taylor, *Sources of the Self*, p. 129.

7 Abrams cites these passages in *Natural Supernaturalism*, p. 85.

8 As Taylor puts it, "By going inward, I am drawn upward" (*Sources of the Self*, p. 134).

9 Owen Barfield, *Saving the Appearances: A Study in Idolatry* (New York: Harcourt Brace Jovanovich, 1965), pp. 32–3.

10 Ibid., p. 42. Italics in the original.

11 M. I. Finley, *The World of Odysseus*, rev. edn (New York, Viking, 1965), pp. 53–5. Finley writes: "The terrible thing about a *thes* was his lack of attachment, his not belonging. The authoritarian household, the *oikos*, was the center around which life was organized, from which flowed not only the satisfaction of material needs, including security, but

ethical norms and values, duties, obligations, and responsibilities, social relationships, and relations with the gods" (p. 54). Max Weber has shown how serfs on large feudal manors were often regarded as members of the household, and how a deep-seated sense of belonging arose from that experience.

12 See Paul Woodruff, *Reverence: Renewing a Forgotten Virtue* (Oxford: Oxford University Press, 2001).

13 Friedrich Nietzsche, *The Birth of Tragedy*, trans. C. Guignon and D. Pereboom, in Guignon and Pereboom, eds., *Existentialism: Basic Writings*, 2nd edn (Indianapolis: Hackett, 2001), pp. 121–2.

14 Mircea Eliade, *The Sacred and the Profane: The Nature of Religion* (New York: Harcourt, Brace & World, 1959), pp. 116–17.

15 C. S. Lewis, *The Discarded Image: An Introduction to Medieval and Renaissance Literature* (Cambridge: Cambridge University Press, 1978), p. 42.

16 Eliade *The Sacred and the Profane*, pp. 69–70.

17 Chinua Achebe, *Things Fall Apart* (Oxford: Heinemann, 1986), p. 85.

18 Karl Löwith *Meaning in History* (Chicago: University of Chicago Press, 1949), p. 185

19 Ibid., p. 183.

20 The idea that this conception of honor no longer plays a crucial role in modern life is suggested by Peter Berger in his "The Obsolescence of the Concept of Honor," in Stanley Hauerwas and Alasdair MacIntyre, eds., *Revisions: Changing Perspectives in Moral Philosophy* (Notre Dame, IN: University of Notre Dame Press, 1983), pp. 172–81.

THREE THE MODERN WORLDVIEW

1 Lionel Trilling, *Sincerity and Authenticity* (Cambridge, MA: Harvard University Press, 1971), pp. 3–4.

2 Theodore K. Rabb, *The Struggle for Stability in Early Modern Europe* (New York: Oxford University Press, 1975).

3 For a helpful account of Foucault's view of the self, see Paul Rabinow's editor's introduction to *The Foucault Reader* (New York: Pantheon, 1984).

4 From Galileo's *The Assayer*, as quoted in Dava Sobel, *Galileo's Daughter* (New York: Penguin, 2000), p. 16.

5 Taylor, *Sources of the Self*, chapter 9.

6 Martin Heidegger, *Discourse on Thinking*, trans. J. M. Anderson and E. H. Freund (New York: Harper Colophon, 1966), p. 50.

7 René Descartes, *Discourse on the Method of Rightly Conducting the Reason and Seeking Truth in the Field of Science*, in *Philosophical Essays*, trans. L. J. Lafleur (Indianapolis: Bobbs-Merrill, 1964), p. 45.

8 Alasdair MacIntyre, *Whose Justice? Which Rationality?* (Notre Dame, IN: University of Notre Dame, 1988), p. 14.

9 Margaret Thatcher's words from a February, 1989, speech are quoted in Richard Osborne and Borin Van Loon, *Introducing Sociology* (New York: Totem Books, 1999), p. 5.

10 Hannah Arendt, *The Human Condition* (Garden City, NY: Doubleday, 1959).

11 Shakespeare, *As You Like It*, II. vii.

12 Trilling, *Sincerity and Authenticity*, pp. 24–5.

13 All quotes are from Christopher Marlowe, *Doctor Faustus*, ed. Sylvan Barnet (New York: Signet, 1969).

14 From Sylvan Barnet's introduction to the Signet edition of *Doctor Faustus*.

15 Pascal, *Pensées*, trans. A. J. Krailsheimer (Harmondsworth, UK: Penguin, 1975) no. 201 (translation modified).

16 Phillip Rieff, *The Triumph of the Therapeutic* (New York: Harper & Row, 1966), p. 93.

17 Simone de Beauvoir, from the Introduction to *The Second Sex*, trans. D. Bair (London: Cape, 1953), quoted from Richard Kearney and Mara Rainwater, eds., *The Continental Philosophy Reader* (London: Routledge, 1996), p. 107.

18 Howard Mumford Jones, *The Pursuit of Happiness* (Ithaca, NY: Cornell University Press, 1966).

19 Dostoevsky, quoted from *The Grand Inquisitor, with Related Chapters from The Brothers Karamazov*, ed. C. Guignon, p. 69

20 Ibid., pp. 69–70.

FOUR ROMANTICISM AND THE IDEAL OF AUTHENTICITY

1 Sigmund Freud, Letter to Marie Bonaparte, quoted in Ernest Jones, *The Life and Work of Sigmund Freud*, vol. 3, p. 465, quoted from Philip Rieff, *Freud: The Mind of the Moralist*, 3rd edn (Chicago: University of Chicago Press, 1979), p. 390.

2 Friedrich Hölderlin, *Hyperion, or The Hermit in Greece*, trans. W. R. Trask (New York: Friedrich Ungar, 1965), p. 23.

3 See Taylor, *Sources of the Self*, pp. 380–4.

4 This discussion draws extensively on Abrams' *Natural Supernaturalism*,

especially pp. 149–51, 185, 199; the lines from Eliot are found in Abrams, p. 321.

5 Jean-Jacques Rousseau, *Discourse on the Origin of Inequality*, trans. D. A. Cress (Indianapolis: Hackett, 1992), p. 22.

6 Jean-Jacques Rousseau, *Emile*, trans. B. Foxley (Clarendon, VT: Tuttle, 1993), p. 66.

7 *Discourse*, p. 14.

8 *Emile*, p. 208.

9 *Discourse*, p. 14.

10 *Emile*, p. 67.

11 Trilling, *Sincerity and Authenticity*, p. 11.

12 My sources for these claims are Geoffrey H. Hartman, "The Romance of Nature and the Negative Way" and Harold Bloom, "The Internalization of Quest-Romance," both in H. Bloom, ed., *Romanticism and Consciousness: Essays in Criticism* (New York: Norton, 1979), pp. 287–305 and 3–24 respectively; Abrams, *Natural Supernaturalism*; and Russell B. Goodman, *Romantic Philosophy and the American Tradition* (Cambridge: Cambridge University Press, 1990), chapter 1.

13 Hartman, "The Romance of Nature," p. 290.

14 Quoted by Hartman, ibid., p. 299.

15 William Wordsworth, *The Prelude, 1799, 1805, 1850: Authoritative Texts, Context and Reception, Recent Critical Essays*, ed., J. Wordsworth, M. H. Abrams and S. Gill (New York: W. W. Norton, 1979), p. 98. Hereafter references to the 1850 edn are given by book and line numbers, in this case III. 144–5.

16 Abrams, *Natural Supernaturalism*, p. 90.

17 Quoted in Bloom, "The Internalization of Quest-Romance," p. 20.

18 Abrams, *Natural Supernaturalism*, p. 149.

19 Jean Starobinski, *Jean-Jacques Rousseau: Transparency and Obstruction*, trans. A. Goldhammer (Chicago: The University of Chicago Press, 1988).

20 Ibid., p. 180.

21 Abrams, *The Mirror and the Lamp*, pp. 21–6; Charles Taylor, *Hegel* (Cambridge: Cambridge University Press, 1975), and *Sources of the Self*, pp. 368–90.

22 Starobinski, *Jean-Jacques Rousseau*, p. 181.

23 From Rousseau's *Annales*, quoted in Starobinski, p. 189.

24 Starobinski, 1988, p. 196.

25 *Confessions*, book 7, quoted in Starobinski, p. 197.

26 Starobinski, p. 198.

27 Rainer Maria Rilke, *Letters to a Young Poet*, rev. edn, trans. M. D. Herter Norton (New York: W. W. Norton, 1954), p. 47.

28 Trilling, *Sincerity and Authenticity*, p. 12.

FIVE THE HEART OF DARKNESS

1 Bertrand Russell, *The Conquest of Happiness* (New York: H. Liveright Publishing Corp., 1930), quoted from C. Guignon, ed., *The Good Life* (Indianapolis: Hackett, 1999), p. 174.

2 Charles Taylor makes this point in "Legitimation Crisis?" as follows: "In a sense, we are Romantics in our private existence, our love lives are drawn by a notion of Romantic mutual discovery, we look for fulfillments in our hobbies, in our recreation; while the economic, legal, and political structures in which we coexist are largely justified instrumentally," *Philosophy and the Human Sciences, Philosophical Papers*, vol. 2 (Cambridge: Cambridge University Press, 1985), p. 276.

3 Anthony Giddens uses this term in *Modernity and Self-Identity: Self and Society in the Late Modern Age* (Stanford: Stanford University Press, 1991), p. 153. Giddens notes that in premodern societies, as in many non-Western cultures today, children live in collective settings, interact with non-familial adults as much as with family, and are raised by the whole village. The view that childhood is a time when the child should be separated from the wider adult community, cared for by parents, incarcerated in schools, and generally "concealed and domesticated" in a "separate province of 'childhood' " – all such ideas are relatively new inventions in Western civilization (p. 152).

4 Leo Tolstoy, *The Death of Ivan Ilych and Other Stories* (New York: Signet, 1960), p. 147.

5 Giddens, *Modernity and Self-Identity*, p. 153.

6 Alice Miller, *The Drama of the Gifted Child: The Search for the True Self*, rev. edn (New York: Basic Books, 1997), p. 5 (originally published in German in 1979).

7 Janet G. Woititz, *Adult Children of Alcoholics* (Hollywood, FL: Health Communications Inc., 1983), p. 99.

8 See the *Nicomachean Ethics*, trans. T. Irwin (Indianapolis: Hackett, 1985), 1106a 21–4, where Aristotle says, "[having these feelings] at the right times, about the right things, toward the right people, for the right end,

and in the right way, is . . . the best condition, and this is proper to virtue."

9 Philip Cushman, "Why the Self is Empty," *American Psychologist*, 45 (1990): 599–611.

10 Robert Coles, "Civility and Psychology," *Daedalus*, 109 (Summer, 1980): 133–41, quoted from an abridged version in Robert N. Bellah, Richard Madson, William M. Sullivan, Ann Swidler, and Steven M. Tipton (eds.), *Individualism and Commitment in American Life: Readings on the Themes of "Habits of the Heart"* (New York: Harper & Row, 1987), pp. 189–90.

11 Richard Wolin, "Prometheus Unhinged," a review of *The Aryan Christ: The Secret Life of Carl Jung* by Richard Noll, *The New Republic*, October 27, 1997: 27–34, p. 28.

12 Richard Noll, *The Aryan Christ: The Secret Life of Carl Jung* (New York: Random House, 1997), p. 65.

13 Quoted in Noll, ibid., p. 65.

14 Ibid., p. 141.

15 Sigmund Freud, *The Ego and the Id*, trans. Joan Riviere (New York: W. W. Norton, 1960), p. 17. Hereafter cited as EI.

16 Sigmund Freud, *Civilization and Its Discontents*, trans. James Strachey (New York: W. W. Norton, 1961), p. 12. Hereafter cited as CD.

17 Dostoevsky, quoted from *The Grand Inquisitor*, p. 12.

18 Philip Rieff, editor's introduction to Sigmund Freud's *Therapy and Technique* (New York: Collier Books, 1963), p. 20.

19 Konrad Lorenz, *On Aggression*, trans. M. K. Wilson (New York: Harcourt Brace Jovanovich, 1966).

20 Trilling, *Sincerity and Authenticity*, p. 11.

21 Ibid., p. 12.

SIX DE-CENTERING THE SUBJECT

1 Cushman, "Why the Self is Empty," and Joseph Dunne, "Beyond Sovereignty and Deconstruction: The Storied Self," *Philosophy and Social Criticism*, 21 (1996): 137–57.

2 William James, *The Principles of Psychology*, vol. 1 (New York: Henry Holt, 1890), p. 294, quoted in Graham Parkes, *Composing the Soul: Reaches of Nietzsche's Psychology* (Chicago: University of Chicago Press, 1994), p. 364.

3 William Shakespeare, see p. 173, note 11.

4 James, *Principles*, p. 309, quoted in Parkes, *Composing the Soul*, p. 365.

5 Friedrich Nietzsche, *The Will to Power*, section 490, quoted in Parkes, *Composing the Soul*, p. 354.

6 Nietzsche, *Assorted Opinions and Maxims* (*Human, All Too Human* 2/1), 17, quoted in Parkes, *Composing the Soul*, p. 330.

7 Graham Parkes, "A Cast of Many: Nietzsche and Depth-Psychological Pluralism," *Man and World*, 22 (1989): 453–70, p. 468; the reference is to James Hillman, *Re-Visioning Psychology* (New York: Harper & Row, 1975), especially pp. 24–51 and chapter 2, "Pathologizing or Falling Apart."

8 Clifford Geertz, "The Impact of the Concept of Culture on the Concept of Man," reprinted in Geertz's *The Interpretation of Cultures: Selected Essays* (New York: Basic Books, 1973), p. 46.

9 Richard Rorty, *Contingency, Irony, and Solidarity* (Cambridge: Cambridge University Press, 1989).

10 Michel Foucault, "The Subject and Power," in *Michel Foucault: Beyond Structuralism and Hermeneutics*, by Hubert Dreyfus and Paul Rabinow (Chicago: University of Chicago Press, 1982), p. 216.

11 Kenneth J. Gergen, *The Saturated Self: Dilemmas of Identity in Contemporary Life* (New York: Basic Books, 1991), pp. 15–16.

12 Jonathan Culler, *Ferdinand de Saussure* (Harmondsworth, UK: Penguin, 1976), p. 82.

13 Friedrich Nietzsche, *The Gay Science*, trans. W. Kaufmann (New York: Vintage Books, 1974), section 382.

14 Mikhail Bakhtin, *The Dialogical Imagination: Four Essays by M. M. Bakhtin*, ed. M. Holquist (Austin: University of Texas Press, 1981) and *Problems of Dostoevsky's Poetics*, ed. C. Emerson (Minneapolis: University of Minnesota Press, 1984).

15 This account is based on Jerome Bruner's *Child's Talk* (New York: Norton, 1983).

16 See Charles Taylor, "The Dialogical Self," in *The Interpretive Turn: Philosophy, Science, Culture*, ed. D. R. Hiley, J. F. Bohman and R. Shusterman (Ithaca, NY: Cornell University Press, 1991) and "Interpretation and the Sciences of Man," in his *Philosophy and the Human Sciences, Philosophical Papers*, vol. 2 (Cambridge: Cambridge University Press, 1985), especially the line on page 40: "we are aware of the world through a 'we' before we are through an 'I.' "

17 Hans-Georg Gadamer, *Truth and Method*, 2nd edn, trans. J. Weinsheimer and D. G. Marshall (New York: Crossroad, 1989), p. 276.

18 Frank C. Richardson, Anthony Rogers, and Jennifer McCarroll, "Toward a Dialogical Self," *American Behavioral Scientist*, 41 (Jan. 1998): 496–515.

19 Hubert J. M. Hermans, Harry J. G. Kempen, and Rens J. P. van Loon, "The Dialogical Self: Beyond Individualism and Rationalism," *American Psychologist*, 47 (Jan. 1992): 23–33, p. 28, cited in Richardson *et al.*, "Toward a Dialogical Self," p. 512.

20 This criticism is not really fair to Richardson *et al.*, because they have tried to account for the nature of the respondent in dialogical exchanges in terms of an ongoing narrative, a conception that will be the subject of the next chapter.

21 Giddens, *Modernity and Self-Identity*, p. 190.

22 Jane Flax, *Thinking Fragments: Psychoanalysis, Feminism, and Postmodernism in the Contemporary West* (Berkeley: University of California Press, 1990), p. 220.

23 See Ian Hacking, *Rewriting the Soul: Multiple Personality and the Sciences of Memory* (Princeton: Princeton University Press, 1995) and Joan Acocella, *Creating Hysteria: Women and Multiple Personality Disorder* (San Francisco: Jossey-Bass, 1999).

SEVEN STORY-SHAPED SELVES

1 This formulation comes from the psychoanalytic theorist, Roy Schafer, *Retelling a Life: Narration and Dialogue in Psychoanalysis* (New York: Basic Books, 1992).

2 Friedrich Nietzsche, *The Gay Science*, trans. W. Kaufmann (New York: Vintage Books, 1974), §290. All references to this work (*GS*) are to section numbers.

3 Alexander Nehamas, "How to Become What One Is," *The Philosophical Review*, 92 (July 1983): 385–417. See also his *Nietzsche: Life as Literature* (Cambridge, MA: Harvard University Press, 1985).

4 Nehamas, "How to Become What One Is," p. 411.

5 Martin Heidegger, *Being and Time*, trans. J. Macquarrie and E. Robinson (New York: Harper & Row, 1962).

6 Paul Ricoeur, "Narrative Time," *Critical Inquiry*, 7 (Autumn 1980): 169–90 and *Time and Narrative*, vol. 1, trans. K. McLaughlin and D. Pellauer (Chicago: University of Chicago Press, 1984).

7 Alasdair MacIntyre, *After Virtue*, 2nd edn (Notre Dame, IN: University of Notre Dame Press, 1984), p. 211.

8 Charles Taylor, *Sources of the Self*, pp. 47–8.

9 For this way of putting the point I am indebted to Joseph Dunne's "Beyond Sovereignty and Deconstruction: The Storied Self," p. 152.

10 Harry Frankfurt, *The Importance of What We Care About: Philosophical Essays* (Cambridge: Cambridge University Press, 1988).

11 John Kekes, *The Art of Life* (Ithaca, NY: Cornell University Press, 2002), p. 21.

12 Jerome Bruner, *Making Stories: Law, Literature, Life* (New York: Farrar, Straus and Giroux, 2002), p. 66; the term *pacte autobiographique* is taken from the book of the same name by Philippe Lejeune (Paris: Seuil, 1975).

13 Sartre, *Being and Nothingness*, p. 33, quoted in Richard Moran, *Authority and Estrangement: An Essay on Self-Knowledge* (Princeton: Princeton University Press, 2001), p. 79. I rely heavily on Moran's account of Sartre in my own interpretation.

EIGHT AUTHENTICITY IN CONTEXT

1 Bernard Williams, *Truth and Truthfulness: An Essay in Genealogy* (Princeton, Princeton University Press, 2002).

2 Williams, *Truth and Truthfulness*, p. 178.

3 This view, only hinted at in Chapter 7, is fundamental to the thought of Heidegger, Taylor and MacIntyre among others.

4 Cheshire Calhoun, "Standing for Something," *The Journal of Philosophy* 92 (May 1995): 235–60.

5 Many will recognize this last scenario as the theme of Bertolucci's film, *The Conformist*.

6 The understanding of our social life that emerges from this account seems to undermine the distinctively modern suggestion, presented in Chapter 3, that because all societies are man-made and contingent, we can regard our own society as something artificial and inhuman, having nothing to do with our "real" lives as individuals. What the description of a democratic society shows is how our contemporary beliefs concerning freedom, dignity and self-fulfillment are so tightly interwoven with social practices that there is no way to separate out the "social" in order to treat it as something "other" to "real" concerns. Far from being opposed to personal fulfillment, we see that our society is a

condition for the possibility of our being people for whom our most deep-felt ideals of fulfillment and the good life can even arise. Such a society demands our respect because it makes us the kinds of people we are. The belief that we can separate ourselves from our social world in order to discover our true selves is itself a socially constructed idea that reflects both what is good and what is problematic about our society.

7 The term "good society" and the importance attributed to attentiveness are drawn from Robert Bellah, Richard Madsen, William M. Sullivan, Ann Swidler and Steven M. Tipton, *The Good Society* (New York: Vintage, 1992).

8 Gadamer, *Truth and Method*, pp. 110–21.

9 Martin Heidegger, *Discourse on Thinking*.

Index

THINKING IN ACTION – order more now

Available from all good bookshops

Credit card orders can be made on our **Customer Hotlines**:
UK/RoW: + (0) 8700 768 853
US/Canada: (1) 800 634 7064

Routledge
Taylor & Francis Group

Or buy online at: www.routledge.com

Title	Author	Isbn	Bind	Prices UK	US	Canada
On Belief	Slavoj Zizek	0415255325	PB	£8.99	$14.95	$19.95
On Cosmopolitanism and Forgiveness	Jacques Derrida	0415227127	PB	£8.99	$14.95	$19.95
On Film	Stephen Mulhall	0415247969	PB	£8.99	$14.95	$19.95
On Being Authentic	Charles Guignon	0415261236	PB	£8.99	$14.95	$19.95
On Humour	Simon Critchley	0415251214	PB	£8.99	$14.95	$19.95
On Immigration and Refugees	Sir Michael Dummett	0415227089	PB	£8.99	$14.95	$19.95
On Anxiety	Renata Salecl	0415312760	PB	£8.99	$14.95	$19.95
On Literature	Hillis Miller	0415261252	PB	£8.99	$14.95	$19.95
On Religion	John D Caputo	041523333X	PB	£8.99	$14.95	$19.95
On Humanism	Richard Norman	0415305233	PB	£8.99	$14.95	$19.95
On Science	Brian Ridley	0415249805	PB	£8.99	$14.95	$19.95
On Stories	Richard Kearney	0415247985	PB	£8.99	$14.95	$19.95
On Personality	Peter Goldie	0415305144	PB	£8.99	$14.95	$19.95
On the Internet	Hubert Dreyfus	0415228077	PB	£8.99	$14.95	$19.95
On Evil	Adam Morton	0415305195	PB	£8.99	$14.95	$19.95
On the Meaning of Life	John Cottingham	0415248000	PB	£8.99	$14.95	$19.95
On Cloning	John Harris	0415317002	PB	£8.99	$14.95	$19.95

Contact our **Customer Hotlines** for details of postage
and packing charges where applicable.
All prices are subject to change
without notification.

...Big ideas to fit in your pocket